Menu:

B.Q. Ribs =   2.75
Meat Loaf =   2.00
Liver (smothered (with) onions =   2.25
Fried Chicken = (Southern Style) =   2.25
Pork Chops (smothered (with) onions = 2.00
Fried Fish :   2.05
Oxtail (Ragau) :   2.05
Vegetable Plate (Greens, Rice, Yams
                               Salad + Corn Bread 2.00

"Vegetable's"

Collard Greens •
Blackeye Peas •
Salad Beautiful •
Steamed Rice •
Home Made Potatoe Salad •
Yams

Extra Veg. = .35

Yams (or) Salad Beautiful = .45

Hot Corn Bread Serred
with Meals
Extra Corn Bread = .20

"Reservation
    Prefered."

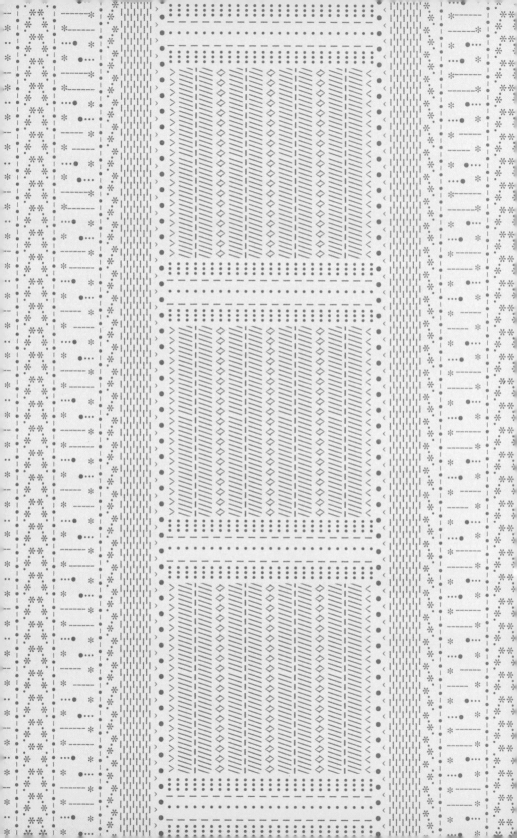

Princess Pamela's Soul Food Cookbook

Princess Pamela's Soul Food Cookbook

RIZZOLI
NEW YORK

New York · Paris · London · Milan

LEE BROTHERS CLASSIC LIBRARY

A Mouth-Watering Treasury of AFRO-AMERICAN RECIPES

....

THE BELOVED CLASSIC NOW Back in Print after 45 YEARS

....

Pamela Strobel

INTRODUCTION BY MATT LEE AND TED LEE

THIS EDITION PUBLISHED IN THE UNITED STATES OF AMERICA IN 2017
by Rizzoli International Publications, Inc.
300 Park Avenue South
New York, NY 10010
www.rizzoliusa.com

Reprinted by arrangement with New American Library, an imprint of Penguin
Publishing Group, a division of Penguin Random House LLC

INTRODUCTION © 2017 Matt Lee and Ted Lee

2022 2023 2024 2025 / 10 9 8 7 6 5 4

Distributed in the U.S. trade by Random House, New York

PRINTED IN CHINA

DESIGN BY Anderson Newton Design

ILLUSTRATIONS BY Anderson Newton Design

ISBN-13: 978-0-8478-5842-2

Library of Congress Control Number: 2016952695

Publisher's note: This reprinted edition contains updates to the original,
specifically reordering of ingredients in some of the recipes to reflect the
order in which they are used.

The SOUL of BEAUTY*

I was ten when Beauty died
And there was nobody,
leastwise no kin of mine,
it made a difference to
if I was fed or went to bed
or next morning
I woke up a'tall.

One thing I knew
was how to cook
'cause Beauty was head pastry chef
"Where the Elite Meet to Eat"
in Spartanburg
and I could shut my eyes
and see her
puttin' together the mixin's
for corn bread, soda biscuits,
peach cobbler, sweet potato pie,
and the best black folk cookin'
in the Carolinas
or anywhere else
Beauty set down her cookin' pots.
Collard greens, black-eyed peas,
chitlins, ribs and chicken,
oxtail stew, and candied yams.

That's how I made my way
by myself since I was ten
goin' from place to place
luggin' my paper suitcase
with a hurtin' heart,
and standin' tall on a Pepsi box
in somebody's kitchen
with Beauty's cookin'
comin' outa my own two hands.

And now with them famous folks
comin' round to my place—
Princess Radziwill,
the Rothschilds and Rossellinis,
Pearl Bailey and Sidney Lumet,
Tom Wolfe and Skitch Henderson,
Norman Norell and Gloria Steinem—
Many more names than I could tell
if I was t' talk straight through
from now t' Tuesday night,
some tellin' me they fly over from
far as Rome and Paris
to enjoy my cookin'.
I feel like they is
kissin' Beauty's hands.

✤ Beauty Strobel, mother of Princess Pamela

CONTENTS

PREFACE*

S oul food, black folk cooking, is compassion food. Greens from the root, and meat near the vitals and the marrow. Culinary genius applied to overlooked odds and ends and to leftovers. Eating, still close enough to honest-to-God hunger, to impart to food a savor deep enough for joy and solace.

The origin of soul cookery is a study of the lineage of the Afro-American rocked from a troubled birth in the cradle of the South. The birthplace, in speech and lifestyle, in rhythm and folklore, is indelibly imprinted with the traces of its black progeny—a bondaged people with a soaring spirit, a *soul* which no fetters could seize upon and wrestle to obedience.

In the ways of culture and of art, separateness is a breeder of a unique creative force. The running brook, diverted from the mainstream, shapes its distinctive configurations from a singular vantage point. And the seepage which inevitably occurs causes an even more marked influence. Southern culture is as much the flower as it is the soil of the Afro-American. For this reason, one may seek in vain the clear line of demarcation between where Southern cuisine ends and soul food begins. The aromas wafting from the grand plantation kitchen and the slave quarters could not help but comingle with the larger-than-life presence of the bandannaed mammy stirring the pots in both places. Pickaninny and white-linen plantation babe alike were nurtured from the milk and the spoon of The Black Mother. And that which, not by virtue of choice remained unschooled and instinctive found its greater encouragement as a loving art rather than as a domestic science. The same deep vein branched out through the hymnals, jazz, dance forms, plastic arts, and cooking of the Afro-American. In these and all of the mundane nuances which comprise a way of life, a common characteristic can be heard, seen, touched, and—tasted. Call it Soul.

This book of Princess Pamela's recipes is a contribution to the taste experience of Soul. We recommend its contents to you with Princess Pamela's own dining salutation—*Eat with lovin' kindness.*

* *This preface appeared in the first edition with no attribution. It is reproduced here to give the complete context of the environment in which the book was originally published.*

A NOTE FROM THE AUTHOR

FOR SOME TIME NOW, nice people who have come to eat at The Little Kitchen have asked me for the recipe for one dish or another. I haven't given out any recipes, not because of keeping any secrets or anything like that. Anyone who cooks knows that ten people can make the same dish, following the same measurements, and it'll be a little different, with the one who has the best feeling for what she's doin' getting the best results.

To someone like myself, cooking is a very personal kind of thing. I still use a domestic stove in the back of my small place, and preparing things about the way you would at home for regular meals. So I never gave much thought to getting my cooking down on paper. But since bein' a guest on television shows, I been getting more letters than I can keep up with. Sweet letters askin' for recipes, and I've been feeling bad about not being able to answer them. I like to think that doing this recipe book on soul cooking is my way of answering every one of them good people for showing an interest and saying so many nice things.

I sure hope everybody enjoys cooking up these dishes as much as I do myself.

God bless you.

—Princess Pamela

Introduction

by MATT LEE and TED LEE

ike her tiny restaurants in New York City's East Village, Pamela Strobel's *Princess Pamela's Soul Food Cookbook*, published in 1969 by Signet Books, almost begged you to walk on by. Printed on stiff brown newsprint in the curt format of a pulp-fiction paperback, it was virtually impossible to deploy in the kitchen without splitting the spine and straining the eyes. Strobel's first restaurant, The Little Kitchen, at 242 East 10th Street, which she opened in 1965 and operated for twenty-four years, was essentially a speakeasy—you had to know to ring the buzzer for apartment 2A. After The Little Kitchen closed, Strobel opened Princess' Southern Touch, at 78 East 1st Street, whose sign boasted, "Cuisine of South Carolina." Customers ducked under a metal roll gate—which always seemed one-third closed, even during business hours—and obeyed the handwritten sign ("Please Knock") since the door was kept locked. Even then, Princess's hospitality might amount only to drawing back the lace curtain that covered the door, a look up and down of appraisal, and a dismissal: "We're closed."

But, as with her cookbook, those who persisted reaped rewards. We purchased *Princess Pamela's Soul Food Cookbook* from a vintage bookseller in 2004—her restaurant had closed in 1998—and our copy, thirty-five years old at the time, arrived already well loved, its corners rounded, the pages on the verge of crumbling in our hands. Once readers get inside this unusual cookbook, Strobel's recipes and poetry—here in near-equal measure—perform the transformative magic of the very best cookbooks, of immersing the reader in Strobel's culinary intelligence, her spunky outlook on life, her lovelorn spirit—it's hard to conjure up a word *other* than *soul*. Hers is a "food soul" that changes the way you cook and the way you think about sustenance.

Given what we suspect about editorial intervention in the recipes, we have cause for concern about the strong dialect used in the accompanying poems. We don't know whether Strobel composed her words in this manner or whether a transcriber rendered them this way. What we do know, from the personal accounts of Strobel's patrons and friends, is that she was proud of the cookbook. The cleverness and quality of the poems also portray a very singular personality, which people who knew her recognize as being pure Princess Pamela.

The first page of Strobel's book, immediately opposite the copyright page, is a dedication—*To the Memory of My Mother*—and beneath it, the book's first poem, "The Soul of Beauty." ("Beauty" refers to her mother, Beauty Strobel.) In four stanzas and a couplet, we learn so much: that her mother was the head pastry chef at a prominent restaurant in Spartanburg, South Carolina, and died when Strobel was ten. That although she was orphaned, Strobel already knew how to cook like Beauty—"the best black folk cookin' / in the Carolinas." And we learn that she traveled north alone, using her cooking skills to survive. The penultimate stanza lays out the triumph of her restaurant and her cookbook: "And now with them famous folks / comin' round to my place," she writes, listing celebrities of the day who've visited her restaurant, including the film director Sidney Lumet, singer and actress Pearl Bailey, novelist Tom Wolfe,

PHOTO COURTESY OF TIM SULTAN

Pamela Strobel, circa 1970

Tonight Show bandleader and composer Skitch Henderson, fashion designer Norman Norell, and journalist and activist Gloria Steinem, as well as boldfaced social-register names: Radziwill, Rothschild, Rossellini. "I feel like they is / kissin' Beauty's hands," she concludes.

According to the author Isabel Wilkerson, whose *The Warmth of Other Suns: The Epic Story of America's Great Migration* is considered the definitive volume on the subject, one of the numerous things we can learn from the stories of the six million African-Americans who fled the South following the Civil War is "an insight into longevity and what it takes to survive the harshest of lives and come out whole." *Princess Pamela's Soul Food Cookbook* functions not only as a superb instructional guide to the cooking of upstate South Carolina, but the confident, positive voice of her recipes themselves—and more on them later— in conjunction with the personality expressed through her verse, offer a portrait of fortitude, wisdom, and humor. Reading this book cover to cover gives insight into what strength of character it took to endure what most would perceive to be crushing adversity.

In *Princess Pamela's Soul Food Cookbook*, the recipes appear mostly on the right side of every open spread. On the verso appear the poems—ranging from a dozen words to two dozen lines—which frequently bear some reference to the recipe that appears on the opposite page. For example, opposite the recipes for Candied Sweet Potatoes and Fried Sweets are the lines: "Now, a pan of sweet potatoes / is sumthin' / poor folks / can believe in." That reference is often a springboard to an observation or aphorism that reflects a life of hard knocks, and the thrill of making the most of the leanest circumstances. Opposite the recipe for Buttermilk Pie, she writes:

> *Everybody ask*
> *me how come*
> *I kin do all*
> *my cookin'*
> *in that closet-*
> *space kitchen.*
> *For anyone been in as*
> *many tight spots*
> *as I have,*
> *sweetheart, it's easy*
> *as buttermilk pie.*

Princess Pamela's Soul Food Cookbook was published within a wave of "soul food" cookbooks. According to Toni Tipton-Martin's definitive, award-winning compendium of cookbooks by African-American authors, *The Jemima Code*, there were no fewer than twelve volumes with "Soul" in their title published between 1968 and 1970. Though it would have been easy to underestimate Strobel's little brown book among the multitudes, her recipes are much more than boilerplate Southern and reflect less the influences of commercial success and pop culture than they do the sophisticated tradition of skilled and mindful cooking in upstate South Carolina. In her spirited combination of ingredients, her specificity, and her steady hand, Strobel's 147

Storefront of Princess Pamela's restaurant on East 1st Street in 1997

recipes—62 of which concern baked goods and confections—preserve and map out the kitchen intelligence of an African-American family, albeit one with professional experience, in the 1920s and 1930s.

This is relevant to us today because the diversity of cooking then—even in the throes of the Great Depression—puts what would follow in the later part of the century, and even our current bounty, to shame in many respects. Strobel in this cookbook parses the mystical differences between white and yellow corn meal, and between fatback, salt pork, and streak o' lean. Her greens recipes capture the radiance of a Southern garden, from dandelion to chard, mustards, turnip greens, collards, spinach, and kale. There are two recipes for coconut pie here, and both call for freshly grated coconut. And the contemporary trend toward "whole-animal" cooking is given important context: Strobel includes a recipe for nearly every part of the pig, from heart to chitlins, backbone to brains, and hock, tail, shank, and knuckle, to name a few. There are three recipes for tripe.

She writes:

> *On Judgment Day I think that the pig will be judged the worthiest of all critters. Ain't any part of him, tail to snout, that don't be put to good use.*

GRANDMAMA WAS STAUNCH

BECAUSE BEAUTY, my mother, was working as an A-number-one pastry cook in Massachusetts, I was raised by my grandmother on Park Avenue in downtown Spartanburg, South Carolina—I was never a country girl. And my first memory is how strict Grandmama was—with *everybody*. In that house, you learned how to mind. Everybody minded, too: her children, my uncles, my mother.

Grandmama was a pillar of the biggest church in Spartanburg, the Majority Baptist Church. You know those cornerstones? Her name's right there. That church and cleaning were her life—and ours. I got in trouble once for washing a hand-kerchief after sundown on Saturday. That was the Lord's time, you know.

I remember Grandmama stayed home and cooked all the time, *especially* if pound day was coming. That's when Reverend Coleman would come around, and you gave him a pound of everything: canned fruit and cakes and pies.

One reason I've got so many names was Grandmama's cooking. We had a pretty home with manicured hedges, and food was always on the table for anybody. But ladies would come over to eat and would be my play mamas. You know about play mamas. That was a delight, and Grandmama would let them name me!

Grandmama was staunch! You didn't think about it, you just had to mind.

—*Pamela Strobel*[1]

Moreover, she envelops these important recipes with verses that express her love of the kitchen, her understanding of men, her self-deprecation, and especially her pride in carrying on the legacy of the women who came before her. Her voice is by turns poignant and humorous, ever attentive to the correspondences between what happens inside the walls of a kitchen and life that happens outside.

Dominant themes emerge in these verses, one of which is her pride in having learned to survive—and excel—on her own terms, and the importance of being a woman of independent means. She advises in the poem that appears opposite her recipe for Molasses Pie:

> *A woman runnin' a business*
> *got no business lettin'*
> *a man run her. It become*
> *a hand-to-mouth existence*
> *with her hand to his*
> *mouth.*

Closely allied to the notion of dignity and self-determination is that of power—the power that helming the stoves and pots, whether for love or wages, gives the cook. In several poems, we encounter the character of a "social-type woman" or a "high society–type lady" giving a condescending direction to Strobel, and Strobel issuing a retort (either spoken or imagined) that reveals her to have the greater experience and intelligence in the subject. Strobel writes:

She poked her head into
my kitchen and asked
me if I cooked my
chicken with a thermometer.
I told her, "Ain't had any
get sick on me yet."

But as much as Strobel is attentive to the dynamics of power, she also manifests an acute sense of humor, typically with a self-deprecating edge. Opposite a page of recipes for Fried Rice and Hashed Potatoes she writes, "If I get to go to Heaven / so much the better. But it's a / comfort / to know with all them hot ovens / in the other place, I / won't be outa work." She expresses that sentiment opposite the recipe for Chicken-Fried Heart, and interestingly references a kitchen implement so essential to her own story: "I have / one / old pot I / been carryin' / around with / me since I'm / fifteen. / I cooked about / everything in / it, includin' / my own goose."

Perhaps the most important theme that repeats in Strobel's verses—all the more powerful for its contrast with the complexity of emotions that the kitchen entails for her—is the reminder that cooking can be a pleasure in itself, in its opportunity for contemplation and the gentle stimulation of the senses. The poem that appears opposite the recipes for Red Beans & Rice, reads "I enjoy makin' rice / 'cause I like the / feel of / it / running through / my fingers / smooth and a glistenin' / pearly-white with / cool water washin' / over it." And in Strobel's world, fallibility in the kitchen—and in life—is no obstacle to enjoyment:

There ain't a thing I do,
a person I know,
a dish I cook,
couldn't be made
a mite better. That's
no reason
not to love it
for the best that it is
right now.

ooking this book is a real pleasure we hope many people will be able to experience—a motivation which is primary for this new upsized hardcover edition. In the current era of deeply prolix recipes, where every turn of the pepper mill is articulated (we plead guilty as charged), Strobel's spare prose comes as a great relief to novice and experienced cooks alike. These recipes are easier to follow for their simplicity, although it helps if you already have a modest confidence in the kitchen. If a true neophyte, you will want to begin with the greens chapter before tackling the pies. And while Strobel may not declare the precise dimensions of a casserole pan she calls for (we assist in filling in some of these details in Editors' Notes), you will discover her reassuring, shepherding voice to be quite effective at dramatizing, for example, even the last detail of egg frying in her Grits 'N Eggs:

> For each egg, place 1 tablespoon of bacon fat into frying pan
> and heat until moderately hot. Break egg into pan and cook
> over low heat. Spoon fat over the eggs during cooking until the
> whites are set and yolks have a nice film.

WHAT OUR FOOD IS ABOUT

I WAS THIRTEEN when Mama and Grandmama were dead, so I decided to go on my own up north—about 125 miles to Winston-Salem. That was certainly North to me. I rode a bus and had three pigtails, my mother's suitcase and diamond watch, and a big white bow in my hair, but I didn't even have a place to stay. So I asked a man on the bus where the colored section was, and he sent me to the worst part of Winston-Salem.

I saw a lady walk by when I got out of the cab. Her name was Maude, and the first thing she asked me was, "Did you run away?"

I said, "No, ma'am." And I kept asking her if she had a room to rent. Finally that lady said she had a mother-in-law in a wheelchair about a block away. "Maybe you can stay there, because she's holy and righteous," she said. And I did, and she was.

Early mornings, I'd go look for work right here by the R.J. Reynolds tobacco plant. You had a lot of little restaurants around there because of those thousands of people. Well, there was this little place on the corner, where a lady had already said I was too young. So I decided to go see her at home when she was sick.

"You're too young, honey, what can you cook?" she said.

I wanted that job so bad! So I said,

t's difficult to know the circumstances under which the book was published and why it was presented originally in such a meager package, but there are signs of injustice beyond the quality of the paper and the trim size of the book. You may wonder—as we do—who wrote the brief preface that follows "The Soul of Beauty" and comes just before Strobel's own "A Note from the Author." The writer seems to be an anonymous editor, and the voice rings somewhat distant and patronizing, loftily stacking up metaphors in an attempt to define and legitimize "soul food"—presumably for a largely white audience: "a soaring spirit, a *soul* which no fetters could seize upon and wrestle to obedience." And yet the writer ends up belittling the subject matter while praising the "overlooked odds and ends, and . . . leftovers" that comprise this Southern cuisine. "Southern culture is as much the flower as it is the soil of the Afro-American."

Having cooked through the great majority of these recipes, we can't help but wonder whether the editorial culture of New York cookbook publishing in the 1960s also served to tamp down the spices and

"Well, *who* is gonna cook the food for lunch?"

Pretty soon, she's send me to the restaurant to help the salad lady. When I got there, I saw this high sink was filled with dishes, and I couldn't even reach the sink! So I looked out back, and there were some Coca-Cola crates, and I kept piling them up until I could reach the sink.

I washed those dishes, and after that, I took the chops out of the icebox, and I made chops and I made steaks. You know how you take the steak and flatten it out and then fry them off and then make gravy? You talk about something good.

I even started making the slaw my own way that day, and pretty soon the salad lady made it that way. When I

started there, I couldn't even lift the frying pan down without someone helping me!

That was the beginning of what I'm doing now. I learned a lot from Mrs. Smith, and I loved her. The only day I wouldn't go work there was Sunday, but I'd go anyway and sit with her in that little restaurant because that luncheonette was her life.

I think I learned how to cook the best food in the world between Mrs. Smith and my grandmama, and I'm trying to keep my place what our food is about. I try to keep the music that goes with our food, the jazz. I have to pay for the musicians out of the chicken money and it's hard. And I sing hard. But I'm from staunch stock, and don't you forget it.

—*Pamela Strobel*[2]

I NEVER GOT A CHANCE

BECAUSE BEAUTY, my mama, was away working all the time, supporting us, I never got to be with her very much. Even when she came home to visit, I couldn't be with her enough because everybody wanted to be with her, and it looked like they were pushing me away.

Even when Beauty got sick in Boston and came home to die, I couldn't be with her enough. She was only twenty-eight. And she had been getting ready to bring me up there. Beauty wanted me to be a concert pianist or a doctor!

I can tell you something. Beauty was on her deathbed, and she called us all in there. And pretty soon she asked for some food. Well, I was a little thing and I didn't do any cooking. But I went in the kitchen and boiled some water and put some cauliflower in and brought it to my mother.

Then she said to my uncles and all, "I have taken care of you all, all these years. But now I want to rest, and now I want you to take care of my child."

I never got the chance to say the things I really wanted to say to Beauty— all by myself, without any interference or anybody around me. I never got a chance to say them one-to-one.

—Pamela Strobel[3]

---

seasonings in the book, to the effect that ingredients like fresh garlic, Worcestershire sauce, ground mustard, bay leaf, Tabasco, and hot peppers are often reduced to mere benedictions, token amounts that don't flavor the dish. (The Red Rice recipe, for example, calls for one-eighth teaspoon of Tabasco in a recipe serving eight people.) Globally, in cooking through this book, we've figured out that readers can reasonably double—and often triple—the amounts of these seasoning ingredients to bring them into detectable balance. In many cases, we have called out in our Editors' Notes a specific multiple suited to contemporary tastes, but we advise you to season to *your* taste and generally to be prepared to increase the spice and seasonings (excepting salt and sugar) from what is written.

The experience of cooking from the book launched us into further inquiry into Strobel's life and impact on today's culinary culture, in which the contributions of cooks who came before are much prized but seldom acknowledged. Information about Pamela Strobel's life—beyond what she offers in her *Soul Food Cookbook*—is scant, particularly when measured by the apparent influence of her artistry and public personality. The few

» – » – » – » – » – » – »

foundational texts we have to draw upon for information about her life and character include Milton Glaser and Jerome Snyder's "The Underground Gourmet" column on The Little Kitchen that appeared in *New York Herald Tribune* on March 12, 1966 (shortly after the restaurant opened). We know that Craig Claiborne was a fan and included her restaurant in his 1967 *Directory to Dining Out in Manhattan* and in later editions. The interviews with Strobel in *The Common Ground Book: A Circle of Friends*, by Remar Sutton and Mary Abbott Waite, published in 1992—a compendium of Studs Terkel–esque oral history featuring interviews with individuals famous, somewhat famous, and not at all famous on various subjects of the authors' choosing—add rare detail and emotion to her story, particularly since these are direct transcripts of Strobel's own voice. And the journalist Tim Sultan's three-page feature for the November 1997 issue of *GQ*, "This Ain't No Theme Bar," is the last published work about her that we've found, and perhaps the most expansive portrait we have of Strobel, since Sultan himself was a regular and a fan of her music, and in the course of writing the story, he interviewed her about her outlook on life, music (she often sang in her restaurant, especially in the later years), and food.

What emerges in these texts is a narrative that shares much with other Great Migration stories of leaving the Jim Crow–era South looking for freedom from hurt, humiliation, and subjugation and for the hope of better opportunities in the Big City. But Strobel's story adds some wrenching particularities. She grew up knowing her mother only intermittently, as Beauty herself had left Spartanburg, where she was head pastry chef at the Elite Restaurant, to pursue a job in Boston. We know that Strobel lived with her grandmother, Addie Strobel, that her Uncle Isaac was also a pastry chef, and that Strobel's mother mainly supported them with her earnings from the job in Boston. We know that Beauty became ill in Boston and returned to Spartanburg to die, and that soon after Beauty died, Strobel's grandmother died too. Strobel, still in her teens, left Spartanburg shortly after that, stopping first in Winston-Salem, North Carolina, and working at a couple of restaurants there for a time, before moving in her later teens with a friend, whom she refers to as a "shake dancer," to New York City. (Census records point toward Pamela's birth names being either Addie Mae or Mary; her birth date was in the years 1927 to 1929.)

Little is known of Strobel's early New York period, in the 1950s, but by the mid-1960s, it is clear that she had established a restaurant of her own at 242 East 10th Street, and that with her distinctive format—serving Southern favorites to a few tables at a time, with a live band shoehorned in—she very quickly built a passionate following that included celebrities and diners from all boroughs of the city.

A year after opening, in 1966, Craig Claiborne first wrote about the restaurant for *The New York Times*, and four years after opening, Strobel published this cookbook.

The power of Strobel's personality, as remembered by the thousands of people who experienced it, was consistent: indelible and electric, an evening in her presence was a roller-coaster ride of emotions that ended either in a rapture—as the smothered pork chop and corn bread soothed, and Strobel took the microphone to conjure the deepest blues—or in ruin, if she tossed your ass into the street when one of your guests brought a sense of entitlement to the table. Strobel had rules of decorum, which protected her primacy in her restaurant and allowed her to construct evenings for people that were personal and special. Time slowed down if you were allowed in the door. She visited with each table. The feeling of entering, and being accepted, into the genteel Southern outpost Strobel created must have been a great privilege against the hurly-burly of post Vietnam-era New York.

Sherron Watkins (who would later become the Enron whistle-blower) became a regular in the late 1980s, and writes: "Princess Pamela wanted only guests that acted like they were in her home. No customers. I guess she was after her perfect audience, because at some point she'd lock the door and tell anyone knocking that the place was closed. Then we'd get that fabulous performance. Although I moved to New York at twenty-eight years old, from Texas, there was something about Princess Pamela's [restaurant] and my insider status there that made me feel like a true New Yorker."

The author/editor/food-world celebrity Ruth Reichl recalls her party of six being kicked out of the restaurant in the summer of 1971 when a fellow guest, Bruce Henstell, cracked wise to Strobel about the lack of sweet potato pie on the menu.

We know that in the latter days of Princess' Southern Touch, the cooking was done mostly by a woman named Ada Spivey, and some

I IMITATE NOBODY

THE CROWDS were there once. When she had a larger space and room for a thirteen-piece band, Roy Eldridge would come by to eat on his night off and pull out his trumpet. Johnny Hartman sang. The younger John Hicks played backup piano for Princess; Lewis Nash, the drums. And not just musicians. Warhol? "He'd show up with two carfuls sometimes. He brought me some beautiful fabrics once. He was something else. It's not my business what he was doing in his private time." Ringo Starr, Diana Ross, Leontyne Price, Mike Wallace—yes, even Mike Wallace is earnestly smiling from the wall near the piano. But ask her about these faces and she'll scowl. Their names are uttered and dismissed with a shrug, as if to say, "Yeah, they come to see me. So? I am the Princess." Or, so she proudly said to me once, "I have no influences, and I imitate nobody."

—Tim Sultan[4]

have said that by the time Strobel opened her second restaurant on East 1st Street, the focus and the glory of an evening at Princess' was as much the music—Bobby Vidal's band (at a minimum a piano and his upright bass) and Strobel's voice—as it was the food. If the multitude of delicious recipes in this book express a Technicolor palette of Southern dishes and food ideas, Strobel's restaurant may have served just the primary colors. But it's important to remember that *Princess Pamela's Soul Food Cookbook* was published more than twenty years before she evolved into a New York institution and jazz icon. In the 1987 film *She Must Be Seeing Things,* by Sheila McLaughlin, a scene in which the main character confides in her best friend is set at The Little Kitchen, with Strobel—identified in the credits as playing herself—and Vidal and his band performing a jazz tune ("Now everybody's worried, since I came to town...") over cutaways to an intense conversation. And in the late summer of 1993, at a party in East Hampton celebrating the fortieth anniversary of the literary journal *The Paris Review,* Strobel and Bobby Vidal performed a set en plein air for an audience that included literary and media stars of the day. Subsequent coverage of the event in the press made no mention of her restaurant or her life as a restaurateur and cook.

But the fact that customers remember her in her later years more for her music and personality than her cooking shouldn't distract from

OLD FOLKS' SENSE

THE DINING ROOM of the Little Kitchen is a typical neighborhood side street store: small, cramped, with a high corrugated tin ceiling. Princess Pamela (a name given to her by the printers of her menu) has decorated the room, which seats only twelve, with cerulean blue walls, black refrigerators, green checked tablecloths, Jewish memorial candles, and various theatrical notices and memorabilia. The tables and chairs are a collection of local donations. In matters culinary, Pamela is a sensitive and authoritative cook. "I always had old folks' sense," she says. She is evasive about her recipes and offers the disclaimer that she cooks by feeling (soul) rather than by measurement. Be that as it may, many say her fried chicken is the best they have ever had. This dish, ordinarily a gastronomic cliché, in her capable hands becomes a special treat.

—*Milton Glaser*[5]

the role this cookbook and her cooking has played in influencing chefs. One food-world celebrity in thrall to Strobel's cooking in the 1980s was the groundbreaking Southern chef Bill Neal, founder of the restaurant Crook's Corner, whose kitchen was the training ground for such laureled contemporary chefs as Robert Stehling of Charleston, South Carolina's Hominy Grill and Oxford, Mississippi's John Currence, both winners of prestigious James Beard Awards. (In 2011, Crook's Corner won the America's Classics Award from the James Beard Foundation.) Although Neal died in 1991, we know that he visited Princess' Southern Touch at least once, and he unfailingly credited Strobel when he put "Princess Pamela's Buttermilk Pie" on his menu. When Bill Smith assumed the mantle of Crook's Corner after Neal's death, the pie remained on the menu for twenty-odd more years, credited always. And Neal's protégé Stehling gives credit to Strobel for the buttermilk pie he serves at the Hominy Grill—which goes considerably lighter on the sugar and heavier on the lemon juice than hers.

We know you are certain to find treasures in these pages beyond her incomparably delicious buttermilk pie, and we hope that as you cook her recipes you will consume her many poems too, small doses of goodness, wit, and wisdom that convey the heartache of being distant from the South and the triumph of being successful in the kitchen.

No two people can cook up the same recipe in exactly the same way. There's a secret ingredient and it's in the cook, not the recipe. That is—lovin' kindness.

1. Pamela Strobel, interview by Mary Abbott Waite and Remar Sutton, *The Common Ground Book: A Circle of Friends* (Latham, NY: British American Publishing, Ltd., 1992), 9.

2. Pamela Strobel, interview by Mary Abbott Waite and Remar Sutton, *The Common Ground Book: A Circle of Friends* (Latham, NY: British American Publishing, Ltd., 1992), 164.

3. Pamela Strobel, interview by Mary Abbott Waite and Remar Sutton, *The Common Ground Book: A Circle of Friends* (Latham, NY: British American Publishing, Ltd., 1992), 366.

4. Tim Sultan, "This Ain't No Theme Bar," *GQ*, November 1997, 288.

5. Milton Glaser and Jerome Snyder, "The Soul of Princess Pamela," *New York Herald Tribune*, March 12, 1966.

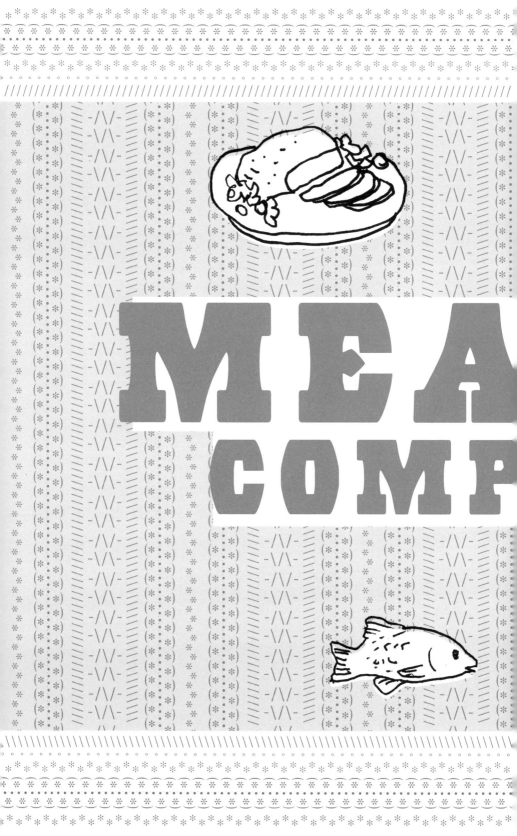

MEA
COMP

TS
LETE

'N OTHER

SOUL TREATS

*She poked her head into
my kitchen and asked
me if I cooked my
chicken with a thermometer.
I told her, "Ain't had any
get sick on me yet."*

LITTLE KITCHEN SPECIAL

※ ※

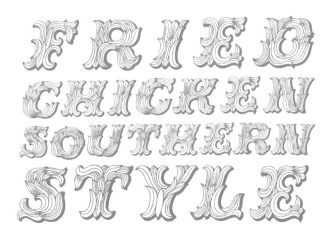

FRIED CHICKEN SOUTHERN STYLE

Cut frying chicken into serving pieces. Beat 1 egg slightly and add ¹/₂ cup of milk. To each 1 cup of flour, add ¹/₄ cup yellow corn meal, ¹/₂ teaspoon baking powder, and salt, pepper, and paprika to taste. Dip the pieces of chicken in the egg mixture, then roll in the flour mixture. Arrange in a wire frying basket and place in deep hot fat*. Fry until the chicken is golden brown. Serve with Sauce Beautiful (page 81).

EDITORS' NOTE: *"Deep hot fat" refers to an inch or more depth of any frying medium, including vegetable, peanut, corn, or canola oil; lard; or any combination thereof. For extra flavor, a piece of salt pork or bark off a country ham can be added to season the oil.

*I have
one
old pot I
been carryin'
around with
me since I'm
fifteen.
I cooked about
everything in
it, includin'
my own goose.*

CHICKEN-FRIED HEART

Trim out coarse fibers on top and inside pork heart. Wash thoroughly in cold water. Cut in 1/4" slices. Dip in flour, to which salt and pepper have been added. Fry in hot fat until browned on both sides. Add a little hot water, cover, and simmer for about 20 to 30 minutes.

*I love gladiolas.
Lotsa times
I didn't have
money to buy a
chicken and
I had to have my
fresh-cut
gladiolas in
the window
jus' the same.*

FRIED CHICKEN

Bacon drippings	Baking powder
Flour	1 4-pound fryer, cut up
Salt	Milk or water

Pour drippings into heavy frying pan $1^1/_2$" deep and heat well. Combine flour with salt to taste and baking powder ($^1/_2$ teaspoon for each cup of flour). Dip chicken in milk or water, then dredge in flour mixture. Brown quickly in hot fat on all sides. Then reduce heat, cover, and cook until chicken is tender. Drain on absorbent paper. Serve hot or cold. Serves 4 to 6.

CHICKEN PIE

Use a 4- to 5-pound stewing chicken, cut up. Place in kettle with water to cover and bring to a boil. Add an onion, a carrot, 2 teaspoons salt, and 3 or 4 peppercorns. Cover and gently simmer until chicken is tender*. Remove bones from chicken but leave the meat in large pieces. Make a gravy, using 4 tablespoons chicken fat, 3 tablespoons flour, 1 cup chicken broth, and 1 cup milk. Place chicken in a casserole and pour the hot gravy over it. Cover with a baking-powder biscuit dough**. Make a few slashes in the dough or cut out a small hole in the center. Bake at 450°F until dough is browned, about 15 to 20 minutes. Serves 6.

EDITORS' NOTES: *Fall-apart tender, about 20 to 30 minutes. **See "Soda Biscuits," p. 169, for this.*

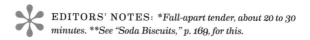

*Every time I been down
I tell myself,
so is the sun—
but he gonna be up high
come early in the mornin'!*

He run like a street boy, goin'
down the alley like blazes—
chompin' on a chicken leg,
his jaws never missin' a beat.

SMOTHERED CHICKEN

Use a 3- to 4-pound fryer or broiler, cut up.
Sprinkle the pieces with salt, pepper, and flour.
Fry in hot fat until brown on all sides. Add ½ cup
of water, cover tightly, and cook over low heat until
chicken is tender. Add more hot water if necessary
during cooking. Serve with pan gravy if desired.
Serves 6 to 8.

I cooked in a lotta small towns,
big cities, little luncheonettes,
magnificent dining
rooms. Everythin' different
'ceptin' my
good soul cookin'. At ten dollars
a plate or one-fifty,
the same pleasure and the
same message—"Eat with
lovin' kindness."

STEWED CHICKEN WINGS

3 pounds chicken wings

1 No. 2 can* of tomatoes, undrained

2 cups chicken stock or water

2 onions, chopped

1 green pepper, seeded and chopped

2 carrots, chopped

1 stalk celery, chopped

1 clove garlic, split

1 small bay leaf

1 red pepper pod

2 teaspoons chili powder

Salt to taste

Cover the chicken wings with tomatoes and chicken stock or water. Bring to a boil and continue boiling for about 15 minutes. Add remaining ingredients. Cover and simmer until wings are tender. Serve with boiled rice.
Serves 4 to 6.

 EDITORS' NOTES: *Double garlic and bay leaf. *A No. 2 can is a large standard soup can of about 20 fluid ounces, approximately 2½ cups.*

*If you wanta know what
kishka is like, chile,
it's like chitlins
and if you don't know what
that is, you jus' plain
ain't been livin' right.*

. . . .

! !

+ +

! !

+ +

LITTLE KITCHEN SPECIAL

CHITLINS

5 pounds chitterlings*	1 large onion, whole
2 red pepper pods**, cut in pieces	1 stalk celery, with leaves
6 whole cloves	1 teaspoon black pepper
1 bay leaf	¼ cup vinegar
2 cloves garlic	Boiling salted water

Soak chitterlings in cold water to cover for at least 6 hours. Drain.
Thoroughly clean and wash***. Place in kettle with pepper pods, cloves,
bay leaf, garlic, onion, celery, black pepper, and vinegar. Add boiling
salted water to cover. Simmer gently until tender.

FRIED CHITLINS: Drain the boiled chitlins and cut into small pieces.
Dip in beaten egg, then in cracker crumbs. Or dip in a fritter batter. Fry
in deep hot fat until golden brown.

*Chitterlings (chitlins) are the small intestines of hog and are available
at certain butcher shops.

EDITORS' NOTES: *Triple garlic and bay leaf; double red pepper and black pepper.
**"Red pepper pods" refers to long, thin dried cayenne peppers. ***To "thoroughly clean"
chitlins is to pick over the gossamer ribbons while they soak in a bowl, pulling off and
discarding any hard or dark spots, glands, or stray muscle clinging to them. Chitlins are
most often available in 10-pound buckets in your butcher's freezer section.*

*When you hear somebody
sighin' and eatin'
with his eyes closed,
then y' know somebody
in the kitchen keep
hers wide open.*

OXTAIL RAGAU

2 pounds oxtails,
   cut into sections
Flour
Salt and pepper to taste
3 tablespoons fat*
1 cup tomato juice
1 cup hot water

1 large onion, sliced
1 clove garlic
1 bay leaf
4 whole allspice
1 tablespoon vinegar
   or lemon juice
1 tablespoon sugar

Roll the oxtail pieces in flour which has been seasoned with salt and pepper. Brown on all sides in hot fat. Add the remaining ingredients. Cover and simmer gently until the meat is tender—about 3 to 4 hours. Serves 4.

EDITORS' NOTES: *Use plenty of salt and pepper in the dredge. Quadruple garlic and bay leaf; triple the allspice and vinegar. *"Fat" refers here to oil used for browning the meat, so use canola, peanut oil, lard, or any high-heat oil that is handy.*

*I figure I
got a right to the
Princess title, 'cause
Lord knows
I been crowned more
than one time.*

B. Q. RIBS

Place 2 pounds of spareribs in a shallow baking pan and roast at 450°F for 30 minutes. Pour off the fat and reduce heat to 350°F. Pour 1 cup of Sauce Beautiful (page 81) over the ribs. Bake, uncovered, until ribs are nice and tender (about 1 hour), basting occasionally. Serves 2 to 3.

 EDITORS' NOTE: *These shouldn't be confused with barbecue (B.B.Q.) ribs and their hallmark smoke; these ribs are glazed with sweet-spicy Sauce Beautiful (page 81) and baked.*

*Though he walked poorly at
   ninety-nine,
he was mighty nimble with his
   fork
and attributed his long livin'
to buttered rum and fried salt
   po'k.*

Fried Salt Pork

¹/₂ pound "streak o' lean, streak o' fat" salt pork*

2 tablespoons molasses

Flour

Fat for frying**

1 cup milk

1 cup light cream

Tabasco (optional)

Cut the salt pork into medium-thin slices. Soak for 1 hour in the molasses and water to cover. Drain and dip in flour. Using a heavy frying pan, fry in very hot fat until crisp and golden brown on both sides. Remove the pork to a hot serving platter and serve with the following cream gravy: Leave 4 tablespoons of fat in the pan. Stir in 4 tablespoons of flour and blend well. Stir in the milk and cream. Cook until thickened, stirring constantly. If desired, add Tabasco to taste. Serves 4 to 6.

EDITORS' NOTES: *Don't omit the Tabasco!* *"Salt pork" is back fat, often with skin attached, that has been cured for long-term storage like a country ham (though not smoked) and is consequently very salty before it has been soaked and rinsed. Streak-o-lean has a ribbon or two of meat running through it, but on balance is more fat than meat, or nearly even; streak-o-fat is more meat than fat, akin to conventional bacon. **"Fat" here is any frying medium, including vegetable, peanut, or canola oils; lard; or any combination thereof.*

The Good Lord say to labor for
six
days and rest on the Sabbath.
If Local 150 of the restaurant
union
got some
drag in
Heaven, I oughta
have a lot of
double time
comin' to
me for the Sabbaths I never got.

SCRAPPLE

1 pound pork (inexpensive bone cut)	$^2/_3$ cup corn meal
2 pig's feet	1 cup cold water
1 quart boiling salted water	Salt
	Pepper

Place pork and pig's feet in boiling salted water. Cover and simmer until the meat is very tender and can be easily removed from bones. Remove meat from broth; shred, grind, or cut into tiny pieces. Discard bones. Bring the broth to a boil. Mix together the corn meal and cold water. Stir into the boiling broth. Then cook and stir until thick. Season to taste with salt and pepper. Add the meat and cook for about 5 minutes. Turn into greased loaf pan. Chill. Then cut into slices and fry until crisp and brown. Serve hot—plain, or with molasses or syrup.

EDITORS' NOTES: *Scrapple is essentially a terrine of pork stretched with corn meal.*

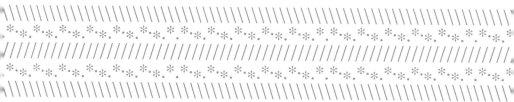

*Practically every kind of people
eat somethin' that somebody
else make a godawful face
at. If that don' tellya what
this race-hatin' is
all about, nuthin' will.
In this life, we gotta give
ourselves a chance to digest a
lotta things we don'
understand right off.*

TRIPE

Place fresh tripe in pot, add boiling water to cover and 1 tablespoon salt. Cover and simmer until fork-tender—about 1 hour. If desired, add a sliced onion or a garlic clove during the last half hour of cooking. Drain, dry, and cut into serving pieces. Serve with tomato sauce. One pound serves 4.

Only place I ever heard her laugh was in the kitchen cookin' over that wood-burnin' stove.

Cut cooked tripe in desired pieces. Dip in beaten egg (mixed with 1 tablespoon water), roll in dry bread crumbs, and fry in hot lard until golden brown. Serve with lemon wedges and tomato sauce, catsup, or chili sauce*.

 EDITORS' NOTES: *Season the egg with plenty of salt and pepper. *"Chili sauce" refers to a product of the same name made by Heinz.*

The most important people I know is the least highfalutin. They don't come into my place like they is visitin' a mu-zeeum and lookin' down their noses at chitlins an' tripe.

TRIPE IN BATTER

BATTER 1

1 egg

1/3 cup milk

1 teaspoon baking
powder

1/2 teaspoon salt

1 cup flour

1 teaspoon melted fat

Beat the egg and stir in the milk. Sift together the dry ingredients and beat into the egg mixture. Then beat in the melted fat.

BATTER 2

1 cup sour milk

1/2 teaspoon baking soda

Flour

Salt and pepper

Combine the sour milk and baking soda. Stir in enough flour to make a fairly thin batter. Season to taste with salt and pepper.

Cut cooked fresh or pickled tripe into small strips or squares. Dip in one of the above batters. Drop into deep hot fat and fry until golden brown. Or sauté in a small amount of hot bacon fat. Drain on absorbent paper and serve with lemon wedges and tomato sauce or chili sauce*.

 EDITORS' NOTE: *"Chili sauce" refers to a product of the same name made by Heinz.

There was this 300
pound cook
they call him
Fats. He used to
have me do the
bakin' and say he
did it. Then one
time there was this
big party
the owner of the
place was throwin'
and I jus' happen
to be late in
showin' up,
yuh see.
Lemme tell ya, the
FATS
was in the fire!

CRACKLIN'S

Cracklin's are made from ham rind or pork fat, cut up in small pieces and rendered of fat over low heat. Left crisp and brown, they can be stored in the refrigerator and used in such dishes as Cracklin' Bread. Crumbled crisply fried bacon may be used as a substitute. Chicken Cracklin's are made from the fat and fatty skin of chicken.

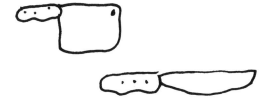

*Fix that man a pig's head
and he'd love yuh
till every day of the week
was good as Sunday.*

HEADCHEESE

Place a cleaned hog's head with all four feet in a kettle with boiling water to cover. Boil the head until the meat separates from the bone. Remove the feet somewhat earlier and serve as hocks*. When head is cooked, take it out of kettle and remove all bone, skin, and fat. Mince the meat finely and add $^1/_4$ teaspoon each of black and cayenne pepper, $^1/_2$ teaspoon dried sage, $^1/_2$ cup vinegar, and 2 cups of the broth from which the fat has been skimmed. Turn into a loaf pan or other mold and cool. Refrigerate until firm. (Of course, the lower jaw, tongue, and jowls of the head are not used in this dish.)

 EDITORS' NOTES: *Quadruple black pepper, cayenne pepper, and sage. * That is, serve over greens with cornbread and potlikker for dunking.*

Folks oughta think about it
when they sit down to meals—
Eatin' is an ecstasy.
There ain't but one other kind
but that don't exac'ly make
po-lite mealtime conversation.

SCRAMBLED BRAINS

1 pound brains*

1 tablespoon vinegar

1 teaspoon salt

6 eggs, slightly beaten

Salt and pepper to taste

3 tablespoons tomato catsup

1 tablespoon Worcestershire

A few drops of Tabasco

3 tablespoons bacon drippings

Wash brains under cold running water. Cover with boiling water and add vinegar and salt. Cover and simmer for 20 minutes. Plunge brains into cold water, let stand for 10 minutes, drain, and remove membranes. Cut up in small pieces and brown in hot bacon drippings. Combine the eggs with salt, pepper, catsup, Worcestershire, and Tabasco. Pour over the brains. Cook and stir over low heat until eggs are set. Serves 4 to 6.

 EDITORS' NOTES: *Pork brains are most likely the intended variety, though this recipe works with sheep and calf brains as well.*

CAROLINA
Baked Ham

Soak a salt-cured ham overnight in water to cover, to which 1 cup of vinegar has been added. Drain. Cover with hot water and add another cup of vinegar. Gently simmer until parboiled. Drain and rinse. Again, place the ham in hot water to cover and add 1 or 2 bay leaves, 3 tablespoons sugar, a strip of lemon peel, and a chopped onion. Gently simmer until tender—about 3 hours. Skin the ham. Combine 1 cup brown sugar with 1 teaspoon dry mustard and moisten with a little broth. Pat the mixture onto the ham and stud with a few cloves. Place in baking pan and bake at 350°F for 1 hour, basting occasionally with its brown sugar syrup.

EDITORS' NOTE: *A whole salt-cured ham—sometimes known as a "country ham" or "smokehouse ham"—is a feast, a special-occasion trophy with intense, earthy ham flavor. A typical country ham is more than 12 pounds and has been embalmed with salt, so it is basically shelf-stable and leathery. It comes back to life when it has been soaked in water overnight, the salty water discarded, and then soaked or boiled again once or twice more, as in this recipe. (The baking with brown sugar and cloves is a finishing touch, to crisp the exterior.) Even with all that diluting water, expect a briskly salty and delicious ham.*

You gotta learn to take the bitter with the sweet.
Anybody knows good cookin' knows that.

*On Sundays when I was nine
there was always lotsa Bible
readin'
and milk-baked ham
and singin' to the good Lord
before the biscuits got cold.*

MILK-BAKED HAM

A 2"-thick slice of ham*
1 tablespoon flour
2 heaping teaspoons dry mustard
2 tablespoons brown sugar
Sweet milk

Combine the flour, dry mustard, and brown sugar. Work the mixture into both sides of the ham. Place in baking dish and cover completely with milk. Bake at 350°F for about 1 hour, or until the ham is tender. When ham is done, its surface should be browned and the milk almost entirely disappeared.

 EDITORS' NOTE: *Standard wet-cured ham available at the grocery store is appropriate for this recipe.*

Fresh pork sausage
is like a sweet prayer.
It may not bring you anythin'
* good*
but it make everythin' bad
a mite easier
to swallow.

Pork Spoon Bread

1 pound ground pork	2 tablespoons minced onion
1 teaspoon salt	1 tablespoon minced celery
1 teaspoon pepper	$^3/_4$ cup yellow corn meal
$^1/_4$ teaspoon ground sage	1 cup milk
No. 1 can of tomatoes (2 cups)	3 eggs, well beaten

Place the ground pork in frying pan and break up with a fork. Sprinkle with salt, pepper, and sage and mix well. Fry until brown and cooked throughout. Drain off the fat and reserve. Combine tomatoes, onion, and celery in saucepan and let boil for several minutes. Gradually stir in the corn meal*. Cook until thick, stirring constantly. Stir in the milk and heat through. Combine the beaten eggs with the pork, $^1/_4$ cup** of the reserved fat, and the corn meal mixture. Turn into a casserole*** and bake at 375°F for about 45 to 50 minutes****. Serves 4.

EDITORS' NOTES: *Triple celery and sage; double onion and pepper; use $^1/_2$ teaspoon more salt.* *Add the milk with the corn meal, and add more if necessary.* **Ground pork these days is super lean, so use bacon drippings or vegetable oil to make up the difference.* ***A 9-by-11-inch casserole.* ****Consider topping with shredded cheese 15 minutes before completion.*

*A lot of marriages may be
made in Heaven but
I bet a darn sight
more been made
leanin' over a hot
stove in the kitchen.*

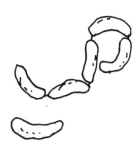

LINKS

Cut pork link sausages apart and place in frying pan. Add boiling water to cover and cook over low heat for 5 minutes. Drain and brown evenly over moderate heat. Serve with any of the following: fried chicken, mashed sweet potatoes, corn bread, eggs, fried apples, rice, griddle cakes, potatoes.

Nobody's perfect.
Everybody make mistakes.
That's why pencils
got erasers on 'em.

HAM HOCKS &
TURNIP GREENS

2 pounds young, tender
turnip greens

1 pound ham hocks*, ham
fat, or ham bone

2 red pepper pods**

Boiling water

Salt and pepper

Thoroughly wash the greens, breaking off the tough stems.
Place them in a pot with ham hocks and red pepper pods.
Cover with boiling water and boil gently for 3 hours. When
done, season to taste with salt and pepper. Drain, reserving the
cooking liquid. Arrange on serving platter with the meat over
the greens. Serve with corn bread and cups of "pot likker" (the
reserved cooking liquid) for dunking. Serves 6.

 EDITORS' NOTES: *Ham hocks for seasoning are typically cured and
smoked a rich mahogany brown. **"Red pepper pods" refers to long, thin dried
cayenne peppers.

Lately I been robbin' Paul, to pay back Peter.

BLACK-EYED PEAS & HAM HOCKS

1 pound dried black-eyed
    peas
Boiling water
2 pounds ham hocks*
2 onions, chopped
2 stalks celery, chopped

1 small bay leaf
1 clove garlic
1 pod hot red pepper
1 small can of tomato
    puree
2 tablespoons chili sauce**

Wash the peas. Cover with boiling water, cook for 2 minutes, and remove from heat. Let soak for 1 hour. Boil the meat for 30 minutes in water to cover. Add the peas, drained, and remaining ingredients. Cover and simmer until tender—about 3 hours. Serves 6 to 8.

*A ham bone with scraps, bacon ends, or pig tails may be substituted.

 EDITORS' NOTES: *Double bay leaf, garlic, and pepper pod. **"Chili sauce" refers to a product of the same name made by Heinz.*

On Judgment Day I think that the pig will be judged the worthiest of all critters. Ain't any part of him, tail to snout, that don't be put to good use.

Pig Tails 'n Beans

1 pound dried butter or lima beans	1 clove garlic
Boiling water	2 red pepper pods
1½ pounds pig tails*, cut in small pieces	2 teaspoons salt
	1 teaspoon brown sugar
1 onion, sliced	½ teaspoon dry mustard
1 green pepper, sliced	Dash of Worcestershire sauce

Wash and pick over the beans. Place in pot and add boiling water to cover. Cook for 2 minutes. Remove from heat and let soak for 1 hour or more. Place pig tails in another pot and cover with boiling water. Boil for 30 minutes. Add onion, green pepper, garlic, pepper pods, seasonings, and the drained soaked beans. Simmer until tender, adding more hot water during cooking if necessary**. Serves 6.

 EDITORS' NOTES: *Double or triple garlic, red pepper pods, and dry mustard; quadruple Worcestershire. *Pig tails here should be fresh, not cured and smoked. **Add extra water if necessary to reduce salinity and so beans can be served slightly soupy—the broth is a treasure.*

I was raised on three "goods."
Eat good, sleep good,
and be good.
Two outa three ain't so bad.

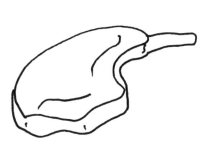

PORK CHOPS
and
CREAM GRAVY

4 slices of bacon	Salt and pepper
4 large, thick pork chops	Paprika
1/3 cup flour	1 1/2 cups milk

Fry the bacon in a heavy frying pan or skillet until crisp. Remove the bacon to absorbent paper. Dredge the chops in flour which has been seasoned with salt, pepper, and paprika*. Reserve remaining flour. Fry the chops in the hot bacon drippings until brown on both sides. Reduce heat, cover, and cook over low heat until chops are tender and thoroughly cooked—about 30 minutes. Stir the reserved flour into the fat and cook until browned**. Pour the milk over the chops and simmer until gravy is thickened. Crumble the crisp bacon on top. Serves 4.

 EDITORS' NOTES: *Season the flour with a teaspoon each of salt, pepper, and paprika. **Reserve the chops to a plate during this step, then return to the skillet with any juices that have collected.

Pork Chops
&
Sweet
Potatoes

Dredge pork chops in flour that has been seasoned with salt and pepper.
Brown on both sides in a little hot fat, then remove from pan. Stir
1 tablespoon flour into the fat and cook until lightly browned. Return
chops to pan and add water to cover. Place a layer of peeled, sliced sweet
potatoes on top of the chops and sprinkle with brown sugar. Cover
tightly* and bake at 350°F until chops and potatoes are done.

 EDITORS' NOTE: *Use a sheet of aluminum foil as a gasket for a tight-fitting lid.

I prefer my meats firm but tender
which goes for
chicken, pork chops, and men.

You play 'possum with that man and you end up cookin' it for him.

ROAST 'POSSUM
with
SWEET POTATOES

Dress the opossum, clean thoroughly, and soak in salted water for 12 hours. Drain and wash, then parboil in salted water, with a piece of red pepper pod, until tender. Place in roasting pan and sprinkle with flour and pepper. Surround with sliced, boiled, or steamed sweet potatoes and add sufficient water or stock. Bake at 350°F until nicely browned.

I get a deepdown quiet feelin'
when I'm cookin'—
like taking a walk
or fussin' with flowers.

FRIED HAM WITH RED-EYE GRAVY

Slice ham about ¼" thick; do not remove the fat. Cook slowly in a heavy frying pan until evenly browned on both sides, turning a few times to prevent burning. Sprinkle each side lightly with sugar during cooking. Remove ham to serving platter and keep warm. To the drippings in the pan, add about ½ cup cold water or a cup of strong brewed coffee. Allow it to boil until gravy turns red. Blend and pour over the ham.

 EDITORS' NOTE: *Standard wet-cured ham available at the grocery store is appropriate for this recipe.*

*Raised for cookin', I always did
have my mind on the restaurant
business. I remember when I was
a little thing this high
hearing about
Noah in a Sunday school
class. I couldn't
help thinkin' how he coulda
opened up quite
a place on the
ark and had all that
animal meat
and no butcher bill.*

BACKBONE & DUMPLINGS

DUMPLINGS:

2 cups flour

2½ teaspoons baking
    powder

1 teaspoon sugar

1 teaspoon salt

¼ cup shortening*

Milk

3 pounds pork backbone**

Sift together the dry ingredients. With pastry blender or fingers, cut in the shortening. Gradually stir in enough milk to make a soft dough that can be taken up and dropped by spoonfuls. Or, add only enough milk to make a stiff dough. Roll out quite thin and cut into squares or strips. Makes about 1 dozen dumplings.

Cut 3 pounds pork backbone into serving pieces and cook in water to cover until tender. Keep covered with a lid. Season to taste with salt and pepper after 1 hour of cooking. Add a piece of red pepper pod if desired. Place dumplings on top of meat, cover, and cook for about 15 minutes. Serves 6.

 EDITORS' NOTES: *Crisco is presumed, but unsalted butter is OK. ** Procure backbone, with some meat attached, from a proper butcher.

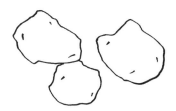

When I opened up this
place I couldn'
decide whether to call
it The Little Kitchen
or Old Mother Hubbard's—
with my
cupboard bein' so bare.

PICKLED PIG'S FEET

8 pig's feet	Sprig of parsley
Vinegar	1 teaspoon whole cloves
1 onion, sliced	1 teaspoon dry mustard
1 carrot, sliced	1 teaspoon celery seed
1 red pepper pod	1/2 teaspoon salt
1 bay leaf	3 or 4 peppercorns

Clean the pig's feet thoroughly. Leave whole or have them split. Place in pan and cover with cold water and vinegar, allowing 1 cup of vinegar for each 3 cups of water. Add the remaining ingredients. Bring to a boil. Then cover and simmer gently until pig's feet are tender*. Serves 8.

 EDITORS' NOTES: *Back off on the cloves a bit, but triple the red pepper pod, bay leaf, parsley, salt, and peppercorns. *About 2 hours.*

*Smother a po'k chop like
you would a lovin' man.*

SMOTHERED PORK CHOPS

6 thick pork chops

Hot melted bacon fat

2 lemons*, sliced thin

1 large onion, sliced and
separated into rings

1 green pepper, cored,
seeded, and sliced
into rings

1 bottle of catsup**

Salt

Pepper

1 tablespoon oleo

Brown chops in bacon fat on both sides. Cover them with lemon slices, onion, and green pepper rings. Mix the catsup with ½ catsup bottle of water and pour over chops. Sprinkle with salt and pepper and dot with oleo. Cover tightly and cook slowly until very tender—about 1 to 1½ hours. Serves 6.

EDITORS' NOTES: *2 teaspoons salt and 1½ teaspoons pepper is appropriate for seasoning this dish; apply half the seasoning to the meat 30 minutes or more before you begin, and add the remainder with the oleo (margarine)—or butter. *Use small lemons, or 1 large. **14-ounce bottle ketchup.*

You work hard
so's you kin
rest and you
rest so's you
kin work hard.
Only way out
I know, is
to enjoy *what*
you workin' at.

LITTLE KITCHEN SPECIAL

Sauce Beautiful

8 tablespoons peach
   preserves

¹/₂ cup water

Juice of 1 lemon

3 tablespoons brown sugar

1 tablespoon butter

1 tablespoon salad oil

1 tablespoon vinegar

¹/₂ teaspoon paprika

Salt, pepper, and
   Worcestershire sauce
   to taste

Combine all the ingredients in a small saucepan and blend. Cook over medium heat until thickened, stirring occasionally. Makes about 1 cup.

 EDITORS' NOTE: *This sauce is a component in "Fried Chicken Southern Style," p. 27 and B. Q. Ribs, p. 41.*

I don' wanta "live a little,"
sweetheart. I want
to live a lot!

Milk Gravy

Use the hot drippings from the meat which you have cooked (such as fried chicken, fried salt pork, roast pork). For each 3 tablespoons of drippings, stir in 3 tablespoons of flour and blend well. Cook and stir until lightly browned. Gradually add 1¹/₂ to 2 cups of hot milk. Cook and stir until thickened. Season to taste with salt and pepper. Serve hot with the meat, with potatoes, or with boiled hominy.

I heard it said that
one of them
French kings,
he used to
have some kind
of medal or
decoration
for women
who could
cook up
great dishes
or sauces.
Somebody
oughta drop a
line to the
President and
tell him about my
chicken gravy.

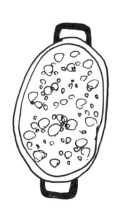

GIBLET GRAVY

When roasting chicken*, use the giblets and neck for this gravy. Cover them with water and bring to a boil. Add 1 teaspoon of salt, a few peppercorns, an onion, and a carrot. Simmer until tender. Discard neck. Remove giblets and chop. Strain the broth. To ½ cup drippings in the roasting pan, stir in 6 tablespoons of flour. Stir in broth until gravy is of desired consistency. Cook and stir for several minutes and add the chopped giblets. Taste for seasoning and add salt and pepper if necessary.

 EDITORS' NOTE: *Or turkey.*

*All through the thirties we ate
so much catfish
we jus' natcherly purred when
we sit down to mealtime.*

FRIED
CATFISH

2 pounds catfish, cleaned
and skinned

¹/₂ cup sifted flour

Salt and pepper to taste

¹/₂ cup yellow corn meal

3 tablespoons bacon fat or
other shortening

Wipe the fish with a damp cloth or paper towel. Mix together the flour,
salt, pepper, and corn meal. Roll the fish in the mixture and fry in hot
bacon fat until golden brown on one side. Then turn and brown the
other side. Total cooking time will be about 8 to 10 minutes. Serves 4.

CATFISH STEW

2 pounds onions, chopped
1/2 cup bacon drippings
2 cans condensed
    tomato soup
2 soup cans water
1 bottle tomato catsup*

1 tablespoon
    Worcestershire
A few drops of Tabasco**
Salt and pepper to taste***
4 pounds catfish, skinned
    and cleaned
4 to 6 large potatoes, pared
    and cubed

Cook the onions in hot bacon drippings until they are soft. Add tomato soup, water, catsup, Worcestershire, Tabasco, salt, and pepper. Blend well and bring to a boil. Add catfish and potatoes. Cover and cook over low heat for about 1 to 1 1/2 hours. Serves 8.

 EDITORS' NOTES: *Serves a crowd. *A 14-ounce bottle of ketchup. **A tablespoon of Tabasco is not too much in this recipe. ***Season well with salt and pepper.*

She sure could cook up a potful,
that woman.
But there wasn't much for her
to cook
an' one time I saw her cryin',
her tears runnin' down in the
catfish soup.

*I bet more conversions
been made by good cookin'
than preacher words.
The good Lord knew it
when he
fed thousands
with that
bread and fish.*

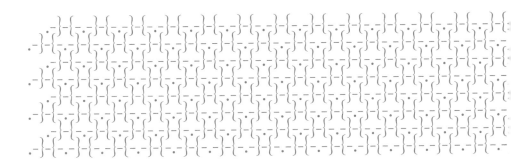

SOUTHERN FRIED FISH

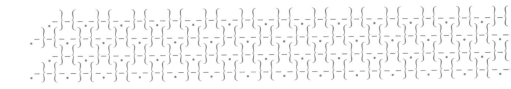

Use boned whole fish. Dip in corn meal that has been seasoned with salt and pepper. Fry in hot fat (such as bacon fat, lard, or the melted fat from salt pork) until browned on both sides and cooked.

*I'm in the restaurant
business 'cause I know
cookin', but there's
more to it.
I love people. I really
do love people.
There's a selfishness
in most and a bit of hate and
a little cheatin'—
but if
yuh keep on
smilin' and
talkin', the
humanness
do come through
and the lovin'
kindness they
got for somebody
someplace.*

Steamed Shrimp

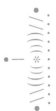

2 pounds shrimp, unshelled	Salt and pepper
4 bottles of beer*	Tabasco
	Melted butter

With kitchen shears or sharp knife make a slit down the back shell of each shrimp. Devein but do not shell. If you do not have a shrimp steamer, use a saucepan for the liquid and a wire rack for the shrimp, making sure that the bottom of the rack does not touch the boiling liquid. Pour beer into the bottom part of the steamer or into the saucepan. Bring to a boil. Place the shrimp in the top part of the steamer or the wire rack. Sprinkle with salt, pepper, and Tabasco. Place over the boiling beer, cover tightly, and let steam until the shrimp turn pink—about 15 to 20 minutes**. Arrange shrimp on platter and serve with cups of hot melted butter. Each person will peel his own shrimp and use the butter for dunking. Serves 4.

 EDITORS' NOTES: *This technique of deveining but leaving shells on is super old-school and very special. *Use a commercial lager like Budweiser or Rheingold. **Shrimp will turn pink in about 5 to 10 minutes.*

Sometimes I feel
about this high—
and other
times I feel
like I'm
ten feet tall.
That, you might
say, is the
long and the
short of
Princess
Pamela.

Southern Fried Shrimp

1 egg	1 teaspoon salt
2 tablespoons cold water	1 pound shrimp, shelled
1 cup yellow corn meal	and deveined

Beat the egg slightly with the water. Combine corn meal and salt. Dip shrimp in the egg mixture, then roll in corn meal until coated. Fry in deep hot fat until golden brown. One pound serves 2 as a main course.

SWEET
GAR
G

ROOTS

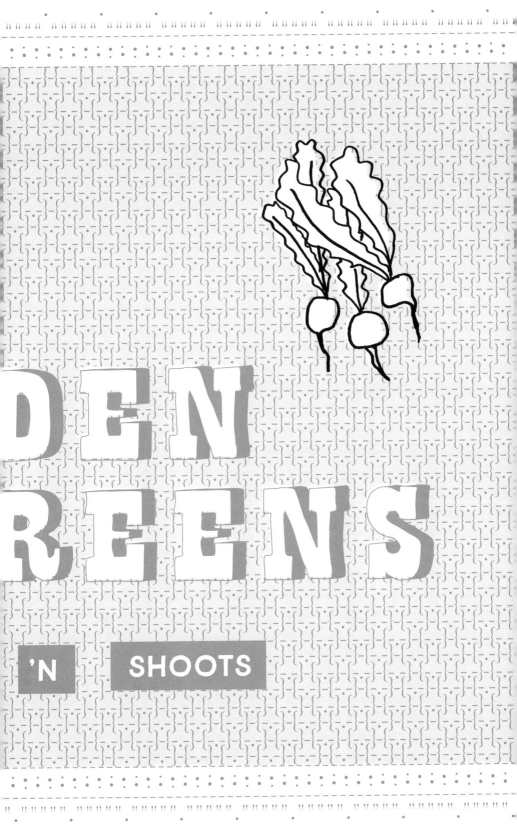

DEN
REENS

'N   SHOOTS

GREENS

Turnip greens, mustard greens, collards, beet tops, kale, dandelion greens, chard: Discard any yellow or damaged leaves and cut off roots and tough stems. Wash in several changes of water until no trace of sand or grit remains. Place in pot and add just enough boiling salted water to keep greens from sticking. Cover tightly and cook just until tender. Drain and reserve the "pot likker" for soups or as a "dunk sauce" for corn bread. Season to taste with salt, pepper, and bacon fat or butter. Or, fry a few pieces of bacon until crisp and pour the bacon and its drippings over the greens. Greens may also be cooked with fatback or hocks, a red pepper pod, and a slice of lemon. Serve the meat with the greens. One pound of greens serves 2 to 3.

No two people can cook up the same recipe in exactly the same way. There's a secret ingredient and it's in the cook, not the recipe. That is—lovin' kindness.

Mixed GREENS

1 bunch collards	1 pound bacon, salt pork,
1 bunch turnip greens or	or ham
beet tops	1 clove garlic*
1 bunch mustard greens	3 red pepper pods
1 bunch kale	2 tablespoons vinegar
1 bunch chard or spinach	Salt and pepper
Boiling water	Green onions (optional)

Wash the greens thoroughly, cutting off the tough stems. Pour boiling water over them and drain. Place in large pot with meat, garlic, red pepper pods, and boiling water to cover. Cover and bring to a boil. Then cook over medium heat, at a slow boil, for about 1¹/₂ hours. After 30 minutes of cooking time, add vinegar, and season to taste with salt and pepper. Remove cover and let the liquid reduce during the final 15 minutes. Drain, reserving the liquid. Arrange greens and sliced meat on serving platter. If desired, sprinkle with chopped green onions. Serve corn bread alongside, with cups of "pot likker" (the reserved cooking liquid) for dunking. Serves 6 to 8.

EDITORS' NOTES: *Take the greens as suggestions; rarely will all varieties be available in one place. *Quadruple garlic.*

Somebody said
something 'bout
God musta
liked the
common people
'cause he
made so
many of them.
I think that the common
things is the
most important
'cause
yuh get
to use them all
of the time.
So it's important to learn
to do them the best. Like cookin'
a pan of great
corn bread, collard
greens, ribs and chicken, and
sweet potato pie.

Collard Greens

Remove damaged leaves, roots, and stems from collards. Wash well, making certain no sand remains. Boil a ham bone or ¼ pound of fatback or side bacon until thoroughly cooked. Add collard greens, a red pepper pod, and salt, pepper, and sugar to taste. Cook until greens are tender. Drain and place on serving platter. One pound serves 2 to 3.

 EDITORS' NOTE: *Any cured bacon-like product will work well here.*

FRIED COLLARDS

Heat 3 tablespoons pork or bacon drippings in a heavy frying pan. Add a pound of prepared collard greens and season to taste with salt and pepper. Cover and cook over low heat until tender, stirring frequently. Serves 2 to 3.

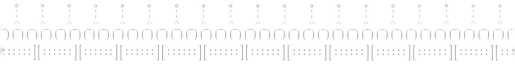

*Turnip greens good for fever
and to calm down
an angry man.*

Wilted Greens

2 quarts greens

1/4 cup bacon fat or other
   meat drippings

1/2 cup vinegar

Salt and pepper

Melt the bacon fat in a heavy saucepan. Stir in the vinegar. When it is
hot, add the greens, cover, and cook until they are wilted. Season to taste
with salt and pepper and serve hot.

 EDITORS' NOTE: *This recipe favors tender greens like young mustard and turnip, dandelion, chard, spinach, and even lettuces.*

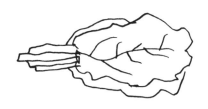

TURNIP GREENS 'N CORN DUMPLINGS

DUMPLINGS:
1 cup corn meal
1 teaspoon salt
1 cup boiling water
$^1/_2$ cup flour

2 teaspoons baking powder
$^1/_4$ teaspoon baking soda
$^1/_2$ cup sour milk*
1 egg, beaten

Prepare dumplings while turnip greens** are cooking. Slowly stir corn meal and salt into boiling water. Cook and stir for 2 minutes, remove from heat and let cool. Sift together the flour and baking powder. Dissolve baking soda in sour milk. Alternately add flour and milk to corn meal. Then add the egg and beat mixture for 1 minute. Drop by spoonfuls on top of turnip greens. Cover and cook for about 15 to 20 minutes. To serve, remove dumplings with slotted spoon to a deep serving platter. Drain the greens and arrange on another serving platter. Pour the "pot likker" (the liquid in which greens were cooked) over the dumplings.

EDITORS' NOTES: *If no sour milk is available, thin a couple tablespoons of sour cream or plain yogurt with enough milk to make $^1/_2$ cup. **Prepared in manner of collard greens, recipe on p. 99.

*A high society type lady
wanted me to manage
her kitchens if I learned
to cook French style.
But I got no use
for a Quisine that
don'
include
the makin's for hog jowls
and turnip greens.*

HOG JOWL & TURNIP GREENS

½ pound fresh hog jowl*

2 red pepper pods

2 pounds young, tender turnip greens

Salt and pepper

Boiling water

Place hog jowl in boiling water to cover. Add the red pepper pods and cook** until the meat is almost tender. Thoroughly wash the greens, cutting off tough stems, and add to the pot. Let cook gently for another 1 to 2 hours. When done, season to taste with salt and pepper. Drain, reserving the liquid. Remove hog jowl to center of serving platter and surround with the greens. Serve with corn bread and cups of "pot likker" (the reserved cooking liquid) for dunking. Serves 6.

EDITORS' NOTES: *Fresh, uncured hog jowl can be had by special request at a proper butcher, but we recommend ordering and using more than the ½ pound called for here— a pound or even 1½ pounds would not be too much in this recipe, which serves 6. Slice the meat ⅓ inch thick and lay slices over the platter of greens. **Cook over low heat.

Dandelion Greens
with Salt Pork

Cover 1 pound of fat salt pork* with water and boil slowly. Cut off the dark roots from 4 pounds of dandelion greens and wash in several changes of water. Add to pork, along with enough water to prevent scorching. Simmer gently for about 2 hours. Serves 8.

EDITORS' NOTES: Plenty of ground black pepper would be appropriate in this dish. *"Fat salt pork" is interchangeable with fatback, streak o' lean, or fatty bacon.

With every spoon of black-eyed peas
He reach over and give her a squeeze.

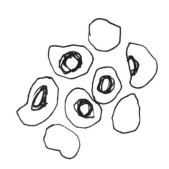

Black- Eyed Peas

1 pound dried black-eyed peas	1 large onion, sliced
1 pound bacon ends or lean salt pork	1 red pepper pod
	Salt
	Pepper

Soak the peas overnight in water to cover. Or, boil in water to cover for 2 minutes, then let stand for 1 hour. Parboil bacon or salt pork for 30 minutes. Drain the peas and add to meat, along with the onion and pepper pod*. Cover and boil slowly until peas are tender. Season to taste with salt and pepper. Serves 4 to 6.

 EDITORS' NOTE: *And add enough water to cover at this point.*

Yellow-Eye Baked Beans

2 cups dried yellow-eye beans*	Salt
	Boiling water
1/2 pound salt pork, with rind	1 onion, peeled**
	1/2 teaspoon dry mustard

Soak beans overnight in water to cover. Soak the salt pork in water to cover for 1 hour. Drain the beans and place them in large pot. Add water to cover and salt to taste. Bring to a boil, then simmer until tender. Drain***. Cut 1" slashes in the salt pork about every 1/2", without cutting through the rind. Place half the salt pork in the bottom of bean pot along with the onion. Top with the drained beans and add the mustard. Place remaining pork on top and pour in boiling water to cover. Put on the lid and bake at 325°F for 4 hours, adding boiling water when needed so that the beans are always covered with liquid. Remove lid and bake for another half hour. Serves 4 to 6.

EDITORS' NOTES: *Yellow-eye beans are a distinctively calico-colored cousin of black-eyed peas. **Onion is intended to be left whole, so it flavors the dish but doesn't contribute matter; thick slices would be fine, however, if you'd prefer to eat the onion with the beans. ***Here, drain the salt pork and cut into two portions.

*Three things I find offensive—
Mean men, back-bitin' women,
and sloppy cookin'.*

SNAPS

1 ham bone, cooked

2 pounds snap beans

1 teaspoon sugar, brown
   or granulated

A few hot red
   pepper flakes

Salt

Place ham bone in pot and add water to cover. Bring to a boil. String the beans and snap or cut into desired lengths. Add to the pot along with the sugar and pepper flakes. Cook over medium heat for 1 hour. Add salt to taste. Serves 6 to 8.

 EDITORS' NOTE: *Push the red pepper flakes, seasoning to taste.*

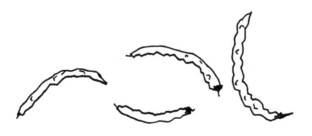

Once I had a cat,
a big fat Tabby,
and he strutted aroun' like
he owned the place. Would
* yuh believe*
it got so bad he would walk
* through*
the legs of customers comin' in
so they'd fall on their face.
I got so mad I throwed him out
* and screamed*
for him to stay
out.
You know how hard it is to get
rid of a cat and I figured he be
* back soon*
enough. I didn't see hide nor
* hair of him for*

a week or two and then I saw
him aroun' the
neighborhood,
but he never paid no
'tention to me and
he'd walk past my
place like it
wasn't there.
I tell you, I
admire real
pride in
man, woman, or beast.

FRIED GREEN TOMATOES
with Milk Gravy

3 tablespoons bacon fat	Dry bread crumbs
4 firm green tomatoes, sliced ½" thick	Flour
	Milk
Beaten egg	Salt and pepper

Heat the bacon fat in a heavy frying pan. Dip the sliced tomatoes in egg, then in bread crumbs. Slowly fry them in the bacon fat until golden brown on both sides. Remove tomatoes to hot serving platter. For *each tablespoon* of fat left in the pan: stir in 1 tablespoon of flour and blend well; then stir in 1 cup milk and cook until thickened, stirring constantly. Season to taste with salt and pepper. Pour over the tomatoes and serve hot. Serves 4 to 6.

OKRA PURLO

Cut 3 slices of bacon into small pieces and fry in a heavy pan until crisp. Remove the bacon. To the drippings, add 2 cups of cooked dry rice, 1 cup of okra which has been cut up and stewed, 2 tablespoons tomato sauce, and salt and pepper to taste. Cook over low heat for a few minutes and add the fried bacon pieces just before serving. Serves 3 to 4.

Feelin' good inside.
Yuh cain't put a price
tag on that.
Lovin' somebody
gives it to yuh
and good home-style
cookin'.

FRIED OKRA

Wash the okra well and cut off the stems. Cut pods into sections about ½" long. Roll in corn meal and fry in hot bacon drippings or deep hot fat until a nice crisp brown. Drain on absorbent paper, sprinkle with salt and pepper, and serve hot. One pound serves 4 to 6.

ONION PIE

2 cups chopped onions
4 eggs, lightly beaten
½ cup milk
Pinch of salt
1 9" pie shell, unbaked
Paprika

Cook the onions in briskly boiling salted water for 5 minutes. Drain well. Combine the eggs with milk and salt. Add the onions and pour into pie shell. Sprinkle generously with paprika. Bake at 450°F for 10 minutes. Lower heat to 325°F and bake for 40 minutes. Serve piping hot.

There's a lot
of trouble
in this world,
a lot of hunger,
a lot of weeping.
And the way I see it,
every home-cooked meal
is a lovin' gesture
and a kind of
celebration in itself.

HOT SOUTHERN CABBAGE

1 3- to 4-pound head of cabbage, shredded	¹/₂ cup sugar
Salt	1 egg, beaten
¹/₂ cup vinegar	Pepper

Soak the shredded cabbage in salted cold water for about 20 minutes. Drain. Pour a small amount of boiling water (about 2" to 3") into a large skillet and add 1 teaspoon of salt. Add the drained cabbage, cover, and cook until the cabbage is just tender. Cook rather quickly and give it a stir once or twice. Drain as soon as it is done. Combine the vinegar and sugar in a small saucepan. Heat and stir until sugar is dissolved. Slowly stir into the beaten egg. Pour over the cabbage and toss to combine. Season to taste with salt and pepper. Serves 4 to 6.

PEPPER HASH

12 green peppers	1 cup brown sugar
12 red peppers	3 tablespoons salt
12 mild, medium-sized onions	Pepper to taste
	1 tablespoon mustard seed
Boiling water	1 quart vinegar

Grind together the peppers and onions. Cover with boiling water and let stand for 10 minutes. Drain. Add brown sugar, salt, pepper, and mustard seed. Add vinegar and simmer for about 10 minutes. Taste for seasoning and add more sugar and/or salt if necessary. Store in sealed sterilized jars. Makes about 3 quarts. This relish is a delicious accompaniment to meats and poultry.

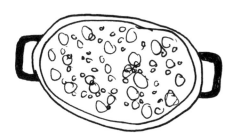

Happiest family I know
don't know
where their next dollar
is comin' from.
Their secret
is that they
don't expect anythin'
and take whatever comes
as unexpected blessin'.

+ +

Shoestring Onions

Select large, thick onions. Separate each onion by layers and cut each layer into strips. Soak for an hour or more in ice water. Drain well and dry. Sprinkle with salt and roll in flour. Fry in deep hot fat until golden brown.

 EDITORS' NOTE: *Two large yellow onions make enough to serve 4 as a side dish.*

RED PEPPER JAM

1 dozen sweet red peppers, cored and seeded

3 teaspoons salt

1½ cups mild vinegar

1 lemon, quartered and seeded

3 cups sugar

Put the peppers through the finest blade of a food chopper. Sprinkle with the salt and let stand for 3 to 4 hours. Drain thoroughly and place in pot with vinegar, ½ cup water, and the lemon. Cook slowly* for 30 minutes. Remove lemon and stir in the sugar. Stirring occasionally, continue cooking for about 1 hour more, or until mixture is as thick as marmalade. Pour into six prepared jelly glasses (see below) and immediately cover with a thin layer of melted paraffin. Use as any jam when serving biscuits or rolls with meat or poultry.

To prepare jelly glasses: Wash the glasses and place them in a pot of cold water. Gradually heat the water to the boiling point. When ready to use, remove the glasses and drain.

EDITORS' NOTE: *Cook uncovered.*

If somebody got me into the
White House to cook up
the dinners for all them
foreign dignitaries,
my soul
cookin' 'd bring
peace and lovin'
kindness to the world
in no time a'tall.

SOUTHERN CANDIED PUMPKIN

Remove the rind, seeds, and stringy portions from a Southern pumpkin*. Cut into small cubes** and place in a large skillet with water to cover. To 2 quarts of pumpkin, add ¹/₂ cup molasses, 1¹/₂ cups sugar, ¹/₂ pound (1 cup) butter, and a pinch of salt. Cook and stir gently until the ingredients are blended. Cover and continue cooking gently until pumpkin is tender, stirring occasionally. Then place in 350°F oven until browned and candied.

 EDITORS' NOTES: *A *"Southern pumpkin,"* sometimes called a *"Cushaw pumpkin,"* is a large buff-colored or striped green pumpkin whose flesh is most like a butternut squash, which makes a perfect substitute here. **Cubes ¹/₂ inch or smaller.*

SALAD BEAUTIFUL

1 head Boston or iceberg lettuce	2 scallions, chopped
1 head romaine lettuce	Sweet green and red peppers, sliced in rings
1 cucumber (unpeeled), chopped	Greek olives
1 large tomato, chopped	Lemon wedges or salad dressing

Tear the lettuce in bite-sized pieces into salad bowl. Add cucumber, tomato, and scallions and toss lightly. Arrange pepper slices and olives on top of the salad and place lemon wedges around the edge. The lemon may be squeezed over the salad by each diner for the dressing. Or, if preferred, sprinkle the salad lightly with oil* before arranging pepper, olives and lemon wedges**. Then dissolve salt, freshly ground pepper, and a little sugar in mild vinegar. Add to the salad and mix lightly. Then decorate as above. Serves 6 to 8.

 EDITORS' NOTES: *Olive oil is recommended. **Lemon wedges placed around the salad bowl or directly on a serving plate serve as a garnish and tartness enhancer.

//•\\(((❋)))//•\\(((❋)))//•\\(((❋)))//•\\(((❋)))//•\\(((❋)))//•\\(((❋)))//•\\(((❋

One way to stop an argument
is to fill a man's mouth
full of good cookin'.

2 eggs	¹/₂ teaspoon dry mustard
¹/₂ cup vinegar	Pinch of cayenne pepper*
2 tablespoons butter	Milk
¹/₂ cup sugar	3 cups shredded green
1 teaspoon cornstarch	cabbage
¹/₂ teaspoon salt	

Combine ingredients, less the milk and cabbage, in the top of a double boiler. Cook and stir over boiling water until thickened. Thin with a little milk. Cool before mixing with 3 cups shredded cabbage. Serves 4 to 6.

 EDITORS' NOTE: *Add cayenne pepper to taste.*

Hot Slaw

4 slices of bacon
1 onion, finely chopped
1 tablespoon sugar
1/2 teaspoon dry mustard
1/2 teaspoon salt

1/4 teaspoon pepper
2 teaspoons flour
3/4 cup mild vinegar
1 2-pound head of cabbage, shredded

In a heavy frying pan, fry the bacon until crisp. Remove bacon to drain on paper towels. Add onion to the bacon fat and sauté until golden brown. Combine the sugar, dry mustard, salt, pepper, and flour. Blend the mixture into the bacon fat. Stir in the vinegar. Cook and stir over low heat until thickened. Crumble the bacon into the dressing. Pour while hot over shredded cabbage. Or add the cabbage to the dressing in the pan and gently reheat*. Serves 4 to 6.

EDITORS' NOTES: *"Hot" refers to temperature and technique, not spice level. *The second method results in a wiltier, more tender result.*

*Crouchin' down behind
the cellar stairs, I whisper
to Leroy, "When you see
him, holler 'Hambone' and
run like hell!"*

COW PEA SOUP

2 cups dried cow peas	1 large onion, chopped
1 ham bone*	Salt and pepper

Soak the peas overnight in water to cover. Drain and place in kettle with ham bone and 2 quarts of water. Bring to a boil. Add onion and salt to taste. Cover and simmer until beans are tender. Put through a strainer, add pepper to taste, and reheat. Serves 4 to 6.

 EDITORS' NOTE: *Ham hock is a fine substitution.*

HAM BONE SOUP

1 ham bone, with
   meat on it*

2 large onions, diced

3 stalks celery, cut up

3 carrots, cut up

3 potatoes, cubed

1 pound tomatoes, cut up

1 cup snap beans,
   broken into pieces

1 cup butter beans**

$^1/_4$ cup diced turnips***

$^1/_2$ cup green peas

1 tablespoon sugar

2 whole cloves

Salt and pepper to taste

1 cup fresh corn kernels

Place ham bone in kettle and add water to cover. Bring to a boil. Add the remaining ingredients, except corn. Cover and simmer gently for about 3 to 4 hours. Add the corn during final 15 minutes of cooking. Serves 8.

EDITORS' NOTES: *A ham hock may be easier to procure and is a fine substitution. **Butter beans may be dried or fresh, but if fresh add to the pot 30 minutes before the corn. ***Triple the turnips.

Four-letter words I use a lot—
SOUL, HOME, and LOVE.

VEGETABLE SOUP

1 ham bone

2 pounds okra, cut in
1" pieces

2 pounds fresh tomatoes
or 1 No. 3 can*

2 cups shredded cabbage

1/2 pound snap beans

1 cup butter beans

Fresh corn, cut from
3 ears

Salt and pepper

Place ham bone, okra, tomatoes, cabbage, and beans in kettle with water
to cover. Bring to a boil. Then lower heat, cover, and simmer for about
2 hours. Add corn and cook for about 15 minutes. Season to taste with
salt and pepper. Serve with boiled or steamed rice. Serves 6 to 8.

 EDITORS' NOTE: *A No. 3 can equates to a little more than four cups.*

GRITS, 'TATERS, 'N

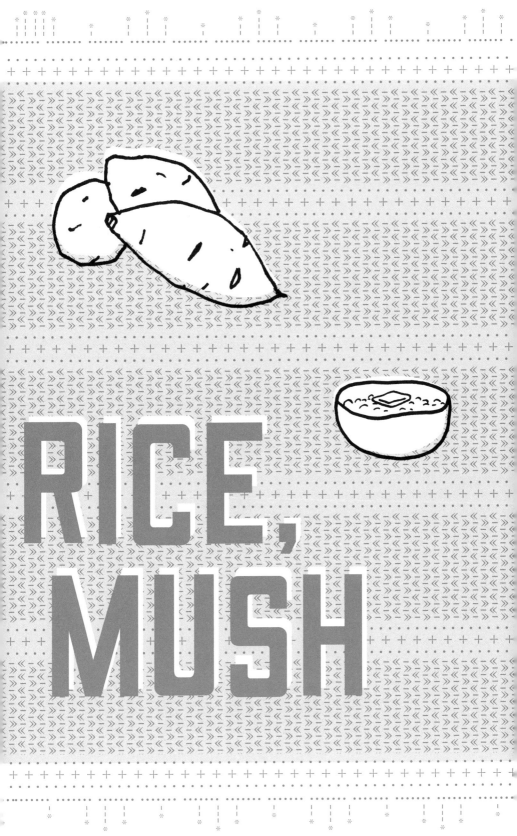

RICE, MUSH

*Now, a pan of sweet potatoes
is sumthin' poor folks
can believe in.*

FRIED SWEETS

Boil sweet potatoes for about 10 minutes. Peel and cut into strips or very thin slices. Fry in deep hot fat until crisp. Drain on absorbent paper and sprinkle with sugar. Serve at once.

CANDIED SWEET POTATOES

1/3 cup butter

2/3 cup brown
   sugar, packed

6 medium-sized sweet
   potatoes, cooked,
   peeled, and sliced*

1/2 teaspoon salt

1/3 cup water

In a heavy frying pan or skillet, heat together the butter and brown sugar until melted and blended. Add the sliced sweet potatoes and turn until coated in the syrup and brown. Add salt and water, cover, and cook slowly until potatoes are tender. Or, if you prefer, place in 350°F oven and bake for about 30 minutes, basting occasionally.

EDITORS' NOTE: *About 1/2 inch thick.

Mashed Sweets

4 medium-sized sweet potatoes	1 tablespoon finely chopped candied pineapple
Pineapple or orange juice	Pinch each of cinnamon, nutmeg, and allspice*
2 tablespoons melted butter	1 tablespoon molasses
Salt to taste	1 teaspoon butter

Boil the potatoes until tender. Drain, remove skins, and mash. Moisten with fruit juice, add melted butter and salt, and whip until fluffy. Add candied pineapple and spices. Turn into a buttered baking dish and smooth molasses over the top. Dot with butter. Bake at 425°F until lightly browned. Serves 4.

VARIATIONS: Instead of candied pineapple, chopped walnuts or pecans, raisins, drained crushed pineapple, or chopped candied ginger may be used.

 EDITORS' NOTE: *¼ teaspoon each of these spices is recommended.

SWEET POTATO PONE

2 eggs
$^1/_2$ cup brown sugar
$2^1/_2$ cups grated raw
    sweet potatoes
$^1/_4$ cup molasses
$^1/_2$ cup milk
2 tablespoons melted butter
$^1/_2$ teaspoon cinnamon
$^1/_2$ teaspoon nutmeg
$^1/_4$ teaspoon ground cloves
Pinch of salt

Beat the eggs together with the brown sugar. Stir in the remaining ingredients. Turn into a greased baking dish* and bake in a slow oven** for about 1 hour. Serve hot, with meat, or cold, in slices. Serves 6.

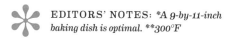

EDITORS' NOTES: *A 9-by-11-inch baking dish is optimal. **300°F*

They come down one at a time
wearin' those big flower hats
and lookin' right solemn
at the cookin' they set down
on the long white table,
like Shebas carryin' treasures
no man ever saw.

LITTLE KITCHEN SPECIAL
POTATO SALAD

6 large Irish potatoes,
  boiled, peeled,
  and sliced

2 tablespoons
  minced celery

1 tablespoon minced onion

2 teaspoons
  minced parsley

Salt and pepper to taste

2 hard-cooked eggs

1 tablespoon vinegar

1 tablespoon finely
  minced pimiento

³/₄ cup mayonnaise

Combine the potato slices, celery, onion, and parsley. Season to taste
with salt and pepper. Mash the yolks of the hard-cooked eggs with the
vinegar until well blended. (Reserve the whites for another use or slice
and use as a garnish on the salad.) Combine the vinegar mixture with
the pimiento and mayonnaise. Add to the salad and toss. Serves 6.

 EDITORS' NOTE: *Double the onion and triple the parsley.*

SOUTHERN FRIES

Wash and pare firm potatoes, and cut into lengthwise strips about $1/4''$ thick. Cover with cold water and soak for at least 30 minutes. Drain and dry thoroughly. Roll in slightly beaten egg, then in fine dry bread crumbs. Heat deep fat to 380°F. Place a layer of potatoes in frying basket and immerse in the deep hot fat. Fry until crisp and evenly browned— about 5 minutes. Drain on paper towels and sprinkle with salt.

This social type woman
she asked me if I
read Ess-ko-fee-yay
and I told her
I'd catch it when they
made a movie out of it.

Oven Fries

Wash and pare firm potatoes. Cut in lengthwise strips. Dip in melted bacon fat or suet and arrange in a shallow baking pan. Bake in 400°F oven until lightly browned—about 40 minutes—turning occasionally. Sprinkle with salt and serve.

HASH BROWNS

Coarsely grate pared raw potatoes. Sprinkle with salt and pepper. Add a tablespoon of minced onion if desired*. For 2 cups of potatoes, melt 3 tablespoons bacon fat in a heavy skillet. Pack the potatoes into skillet and cook over low heat until the potatoes are tender and browned on the bottom (about 30 minutes). Invert onto serving platter so that the brown crust is on top, or fold like an omelet.

 EDITORS' NOTE: *You desire 2 tablespoons onion for 2 cups of potatoes.

*If I get to go to Heaven
so much the better. But it's a
comfort
to know with all them hot ovens
in the other place, I
won't be outa work.*

HASHED POTATOES

2 tablespoons finely
chopped onion

2 tablespoons butter
or oleo

2 tablespoons sifted flour

Salt and pepper

2 cups milk

2 cups boiled, diced
potatoes

Fry the onion in butter or oleo until tender. Stir in the flour until well blended. Season to taste with salt and pepper. Stir in the milk and cook until thickened, stirring constantly. Add potatoes and heat through. Serves 2.

FRIED RICE

4 strips bacon, cut into
   small pieces

1 tablespoon minced onion

1 tablespoon minced
   green pepper

1 cup raw rice

2¹/₂ cups boiling water

Salt and pepper to taste

Fry the bacon in a heavy saucepan or frying pan until crisp. Remove.
Add onion and green pepper to the drippings and cook until the onion is
golden brown. Add the rice. Cook and stir over low heat until it is lightly
browned, taking care not to burn it. Add the boiling water, salt, and
pepper. Cover and cook over very low heat until all the liquid is absorbed.
Remove cover and let stand until dry and fluffy. Add fried bacon pieces
and toss lightly with fork. Serves 4.

 EDITORS' NOTE: *Double green pepper and onion.*

I enjoy makin' rice
'cause I like the
feel of it
running through
my fingers
smooth and a glistenin'
pearly-white with
cool water washin'
over it.

SOUTHERN DRY RICE

1 cup rice	2 tablespoons butter
1/2 teaspoon salt	1 teaspoon lemon juice
1 1/2 cups water	

Wash the rice in three or four changes of water. Place in a heavy saucepan along with remaining ingredients. Cover tightly and quickly bring to a boil. Stir once with a fork and replace lid. Reduce heat and cook very slowly until the liquid has been absorbed—about 20 minutes. Toss lightly with fork. Serves 4.

RED BEANS & RICE

1 pound dried red beans	1 teaspoon salt
1/2 pound ham or salt pork	1/2 teaspoon pepper
1 onion, whole or chopped	2 cups dry boiled or
1 clove of garlic (optional)*	steamed rice (see above)

Soak the beans overnight in cold water to cover. Or boil for 2 minutes and let stand for 1 hour. Drain. Place beans in pot with water to cover. Bring to a boil. Then add onion and garlic and simmer until beans are tender but not mushy. Add salt and pepper when beans are about half done. Add the rice, mix and cook over very low heat for about 10 minutes. Serves 6 to 8.

EDITORS' NOTE: *Double or triple the garlic.*

I don't mind caterin' to a man
*   sometimes*
but a man-woman thing
ain't supposed to be a
caterin' business.

RED RICE

¹/₄ pound sliced bacon	2 cups canned tomatoes
1 onion, chopped	1 stalk celery, diced
2 cups raw rice, washed several times and drained	Salt and pepper to taste
	¹/₈ teaspoon Tabasco*

In a large, heavy frying pan, fry the bacon until crisp. Remove bacon and set aside. Cook the onion in the bacon drippings until tender. Stir in the rice. Then add tomatoes, celery, crumbled bacon, and seasonings. Cook for about 10 minutes. Turn into a casserole and cover tightly. Bake in 350°F oven for about 1 hour, stirring occasionally. Serves 6 to 8.

 EDITORS' NOTE: *Quadruple the Tabasco.*

Hopping John

1 cup black-eyed peas

1 ham knuckle, or ¼ pound salt pork, diced*

1 green pepper, seeded and chopped

1 onion, chopped

1 cup uncooked rice

1 tablespoon butter

Pinch of cayenne pepper

Salt and pepper

Soak the peas overnight in water to cover. If using ham knuckle, place in pot with onion, green pepper, and water to cover. Simmer for 2 hours. (Salt pork need not be "precooked.") Add the peas, drained, and simmer until they are tender. Steam the rice separately until it is dry and "flaky." When the peas are done and the water has cooked very low, add the steamed rice, butter, cayenne, and salt and pepper to taste. Cook over very low heat until all the liquid is absorbed. Serves 4 to 6**.

 EDITORS' NOTES: *Bacon is a fine substitute. **Serves 4.

*A tasty dish of mornin' grits
can put a shine on a man's shoes.*

GRITS

2 tablespoons butter

1 teaspoon salt

5 cups boiling water

1 cup hominy grits*

Add butter and salt to the boiling water. Slowly stir in the grits. Cover and cook slowly for about 30 to 40 minutes, stirring frequently**. Serve for breakfast or with fried meat and gravy at dinner. Serves 4 to 6.

EDITORS' NOTES: *"Hominy grits" is often used in South Carolina as a colloquial term for white corn grits (not to be confused with hominy—nixtamalized corn). **And adding water as necessary to achieve a stiff consistency without scorching.

× ×

SOUTHERN BAKED GRITS

Salt

Boiling water

1 cup hominy grits*

2 cups milk

1 egg, slightly beaten

4 tablespoons oleo**

1 tablespoon sugar

In the top of a double boiler, bring 1^1/$_2$ cups salted water to a boil over direct heat. Stir in the grits and boil for about 2 minutes. Place over hot water and cook until thick. Stir in 1 cup milk and cook for 1 hour. Add the remaining milk, egg, oleo, and sugar. Pour into a greased casserole and bake at 350°F for about 30 to 45 minutes. Serves 6.

EDITORS' NOTES: *"Hominy grits" is often used in South Carolina as a colloquial term for white corn grits (not to be confused with hominy—nixtamalized corn). **Unsalted butter is a fine substitute for oleo (margarine).

Every failure has got a piece
of success in it. It ain't
easy to build success
Outa bits and pieces
like makin' a tasty dish outa
leftovers. But it
is the sweetest and
most satisfyin'
cookin' there is.

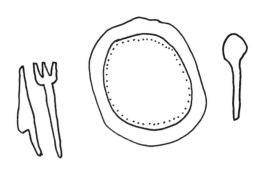

HOMINY CAKES

Shape cold, boiled hominy grits (see page 141) into small patties. Dip in flour and fry in bacon fat.

— — — — — · — — — — — + — — — — — · — — — —

Grits 'n Eggs

Use a heavy frying pan. For each egg, place 1 tablespoon of bacon fat into frying pan and heat until moderately hot. Break egg into pan and cook over low heat. Spoon fat over the eggs during cooking until the whites are set and yolks have a nice film. Serve with hot cooked grits (see page 141). Fried bacon, ham, or links are a delicious accompaniment.

*The most important word
in any language
is respect.
It says it all.
To get it, first yuh
got to have some
for yourself and
what you do in
this world. I cook
and I do
it good as I know
how.*

CORN MEAL MUSH

1 teaspoon salt
4 cups boiling water
1 cup corn meal

Add salt to the boiling water. Then add corn meal, a little at a time, stirring constantly. Boil for about 5 minutes. Then cook in the top of double boiler over hot water until the mush is thoroughly cooked*. When ready to serve, add a little hot water and beat until the mixture is creamy. Serve as a breakfast cereal.

 EDITORS' NOTE: *About 30 minutes, or until the consistency is thickened.

FRIED CORN MEAL MUSH

Make Corn Meal Mush according to above recipe, but using 1 cup less water. Pack into a greased loaf pan and chill until firm. Cut into $1/2$" slices, dip in flour, and brown on both sides in bacon fat. Serve hot, with molasses or maple syrup, for breakfast, as dessert, or with ham, chicken, pork, or sausages for dinner.

Batter

'A'

BAKING
SODA

Butter

*I get as nervous as watchin'
my corn bread risin' too
fast, with everything
happenin' to
me sort of
overnight.*

LITTLE KITCHEN SPECIAL

CORN BREAD

2 cups buttermilk	1 teaspoon salt
2 eggs	1 tablespoon melted butter
1 teaspoon baking soda	Drop of vanilla extract
2 cups yellow corn meal	
2 teaspoons sugar	

Beat together the buttermilk, eggs, and baking soda. Beat in the corn meal, sugar, salt, melted butter, and vanilla. Pour into a buttered baking pan* and bake at 450°F for about 20 minutes. Cut in squares and serve piping hot with butter.

 EDITORS' NOTE: *A 9-by-13-inch pan is optimal.

Makin' corn bread is like
makin' love.
No matter where you do it
it's called the same thing
but how you do it
makes a heap o' difference.

Skillet Corn Bread

³/₄ teaspoon baking soda

1¹/₂ cups buttermilk

2 cups corn meal, sifted

1 teaspoon salt

1 egg

1 tablespoon melted
bacon fat

Dissolve soda in buttermilk. Mix the corn meal with salt, egg, and buttermilk. Add hot melted bacon fat. Pour into greased iron skillet* and bake at 375°F until done. Cut in wedges.

 EDITORS' NOTE: *Preheat the greased skillet in the oven until grease smokes, then add the batter to the skillet and bake.

*I been close to Jewish
people and Eye-talians
all my life. There is the kind of
love in them that
comes of bein' hurt
and healed a thousand
times.*

MOLASSES CORN CAKE

1 cup corn meal

1 cup flour

3 teaspoons baking
    powder

$^1/_2$ teaspoon salt

$^1/_4$ cup molasses

1 cup milk

1 egg, well beaten

2 tablespoons bacon fat,
    melted

Sift together the dry ingredients. Add the remaining ingredients and pour into greased square baking pan. Bake at 450°F for about 15 to 20 minutes.

You kin *keep a good man down—
all you have to do is to thicken
the batter!*

HOE
CAKE

2 cups sifted corn meal	1 teaspoon salt
2 cups cold water	$^1/_4$ teaspoon baking soda

Mix together all the ingredients. Bake on hot, well-greased bread hoe
or iron frying pan on top of stove over medium heat. When browned on
the bottom, turn over and cook until done—about 15 to 20 minutes.

With all them famous folks comin' round to my place, they always advisin' me, "Pam, be sure to always be yourself." Never knew anybody could be otherwise.

CORN STICKS

2 cups corn meal	1 cup milk
2 teaspoons baking powder	1 tablespoon lard or bacon fat, melted
1/2 teaspoon salt	1 egg, well beaten

Sift together the dry ingredients. Stir in milk and melted lard. Add the egg. Turn into greased corn-stick pans and bake in preheated 425°F oven until done.

My uncle used to tell me,
early to bed, early to rise,
make a man *healthy,*
wealthy, and wise.
I been followin' that routine
all my life and I kin
tellya that
all it does for a woman,
is to make her tired,
poor, and not too bright.

CORN BREAD DRESSING

3 cups coarsely crumbled corn bread (see page 149)	2 eggs, slightly beaten
1 cup stale wheat-bread crumbs	Chicken stock
3 stalks celery, finely chopped	Salt and pepper
1 large onion, finely chopped	Pinch of sage or poultry seasoning (optional)
	Bacon strips

Combine crumbled breads in mixing bowl. Add celery and onion and toss
to combine. Add eggs and mix thoroughly. Add stock until the mixture
is quite moist. Add salt and pepper to taste and, if desired, the sage or
poultry seasoning. Turn into a greased baking pan and lay several strips
of bacon over the top. Bake at 400°F until bacon is crisp, about 15 minutes.
Serves 6.

Kids come aroun'
to my place
waitin' to get
some milk and
corn bread. Seein'
them pinched in
faces is
like lookin'
into the mirror
of yesterday.

CORN CAKES

3 tablespoons flour

2 tablespoons milk

1/2 teaspoon salt

1 egg, well beaten

1 1/2 cups whole corn kernels*

Fat for frying

Combine flour, milk, salt, and egg. Beat until smooth and thoroughly blended. Add the corn and mix well. Drop from spoon into hot shallow fat and fry until golden brown on both sides. Serves 4.

 EDITORS' NOTE: *Fresh corn cut off the cob.*

I came to New York with
a real pretty black
doll, a shake dancer.
And when she couldn'
get any work
shakin' in
nightclubs, she
would shake in
my kitchen, mixin'
up the smoothest batter
yuh ever saw!
It ain't what you do
but how you do it.

BATTER BREAD

2 eggs	$1/2$ teaspoon salt
1 cup white corn meal, sifted	$1/2$ teaspoon baking powder
1 pint buttermilk	$1/2$ teaspoon baking soda
1 teaspoon sugar	3 tablespoons butter

Beat the eggs until light. Then beat in the corn meal, buttermilk, sugar, salt, baking powder, and soda. Melt the butter in a deep baking dish and swirl it around until bottom and sides are evenly coated. Pour in the batter and bake at 350°F for about 30 to 40 minutes. Serve hot with butter or gravy. Serves 4 to 6.

Sometimes I get jus' plain tired of bein' tired.

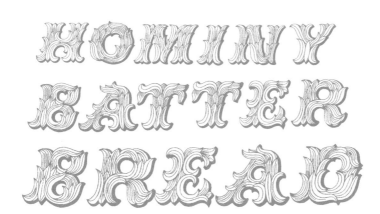

HOMINY BATTER BREAD

1 egg

1 cup white corn meal

½ cup cold, cooked
hominy grits
(see page 141)

1 teaspoon salt

1 teaspoon sugar

1 teaspoon baking
powder

Milk or boiling water

1 tablespoon bacon fat
or lard

Beat the egg until light. Add the corn meal, grits, salt, sugar, and baking powder. Stir in enough milk or boiling water until the batter is as thick as custard*. Melt the bacon fat or lard in a deep baking dish or casserole. Pour in the batter and bake at 350°F for about 40 minutes. Serves 4.

 EDITORS' NOTE: *Approximately ¼ cup milk.

*A lot of them smart sayin's
ain't so smart. Like
if at first yuh don't succeed.
   Many's the time,
in this
world, your batter goes
in that oven once.*

Southern Egg Bread

2 cups water-ground*
  corn meal

1 tablespoon sugar

1 teaspoon salt

¹/₄ cup bacon fat

¹/₂ teaspoon baking soda

2 cups buttermilk

2 eggs, well beaten

2 teaspoons
  baking powder

Sift together the corn meal, sugar, and salt. Melt the bacon fat in heavy skillet in which bread is to be baked. Dissolve baking soda in buttermilk. Slowly and alternately add the melted fat and buttermilk to corn-meal mixture. Beat vigorously for a moment. Then fold in eggs and, last, the baking powder. Pour into the greased skillet and bake at 450°F for about 20 to 30 minutes. Cut in wedges and serve hot.

EDITORS' NOTE: *"Water-ground" refers to the highest quality, most earnest corn meal you are able to obtain; yellow corn meal is implied, but white would be OK too.

*I like cookin' because
yuh kin
see it through from plannin'
to doin', feeding people,
havin' them enjoy
it all in a matter
of hours. Ain't many
things in this life
you start out
knowin' how it's
gonna turn out.*

Oatmeal Molasses Bread

2 cups boiling water	2 teaspoons salt
1 cup rolled oats	1 package yeast
$^1/_2$ cup light molasses	$^1/_2$ cup lukewarm water
1 tablespoon shortening	4$^1/_2$ cups sifted flour

Stir together the boiling water and rolled oats and let stand for 1 hour. Add the molasses, shortening, and salt. Dissolve yeast in lukewarm water and add to the oatmeal mixture. Add the flour and mix thoroughly. Let rise until double. Shape into two loaves and place in greased pans. Again let rise until almost double. Bake at 350°F until brown—about 50 to 60 minutes.

Soul food is kind of a feelin'
about whatcha eatin' as much as
the style of cookin'. This bit in my
scrapbook tell it like it is:
"That black face, black and
shinin'
Coal-black and lit up with
smilin'
Smackin' those spoonbread lips
like everything in the world
had a grand taste."

SPOON BREAD

1 cup sifted yellow corn meal	3 tablespoons melted butter or oleo
4 cups milk	1/2 teaspoon salt
	4 eggs, well beaten

Blend the corn meal with 1 cup milk. Stir in remaining milk. Cook and
stir over moderate heat until the mixture thickens. Add melted butter
or oleo and salt, then fold in the eggs. Pour into greased baking pan or
casserole and bake at 400°F for about 25 to 30 minutes. Serves 6 to 8.

Beauty could make biscuits so light they float right outa the oven.

SODA BISCUITS

2 cups flour	2 tablespoons lard
2 teaspoons cream of tartar	¹/₂ teaspoon baking soda
¹/₂ teaspoon salt	1 cup milk

Combine flour with cream of tartar and salt and sift together into mixing bowl. Cut in the lard*. Dissolve soda in milk and stir into the flour mixture, mixing as little as possible. Turn out onto floured surface and roll out to 1" thickness. Cut into rounds with biscuit cutter and arrange on greased baking sheet. Bake at 450°F until lightly browned.

 EDITORS' NOTES: *Craig Claiborne raved about these. *Cut in the cold lard with a pastry blender, fork, two knives, or pinching fingertips.*

*I'm one of those
high-strung types,
most of the time too
busy to eat. Then
once in a while I
get real hungry and
I go at my own cookin'
like I never et it before.
Then I'm surprised to find
out that
I'm about as good as
everybody been tellin' me!*

Sweet Potato Biscuits

2 cups sifted flour	2 tablespoons brown sugar
3 teaspoons baking powder	1/2 cup melted oleo*
1 teaspoon salt	1/2 teaspoon baking soda
1 cup boiled and mashed sweet potatoes	3/4 cup buttermilk

Combine sifted flour, baking powder, and salt and sift together into mixing bowl. Combine mashed sweet potatoes with brown sugar and oleo and beat until well blended and fluffy. Dissolve baking soda in buttermilk. Alternately add buttermilk and sweet potato mixture to dry ingredients, stirring only until moist but mixing as little as possible. Turn out onto floured surface and roll out. Cut into rounds with biscuit cutter, arrange on ungreased baking sheet, and bake at 425°F for about 15 minutes.

 EDITORS' NOTE: *Unsalted butter makes a fine substitute for oleo (margarine).

*Makin' up a new recipe is a
lot like a song
'cept you cain't give
     indigestion to
an eardrum.*

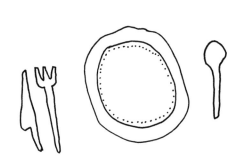

Cracklin'
Biscuits

2 teaspoons double-acting or 4 teaspoons single-acting baking powder	3 tablespoons rendered fat, chilled
Salt to taste	1/4 cup cracklin's, chilled (see page 51)
2 cups sifted flour	Milk

Add baking powder and salt to the sifted flour and sift three times. Cut in the cold fat with a pastry blender, fork, two knives, or fingertips. Add cracklin's and mix just enough to evenly distribute them. Add enough milk to make a dough that is soft but not sticky, mixing as little as possible. Turn out onto lightly floured surface and knead very gently for a minute or so. Then pat or roll out to a 1/2" thickness. Cut into rounds with biscuit cutter and arrange on greased baking sheet about 1" apart. Bake at 450°F until golden brown—about 12 to 15 minutes. Serve hot. Makes about 1 dozen biscuits.

CHICKEN CRACKLIN' BISCUITS: Use the fat from a chicken to make the cracklin's and the resultant rendered fat.
PORK CRACKLIN' BISCUITS: Use pork fat for preparing the cracklin's and fat.
HAM CRACKLIN' BISCUITS: Use the fat skin of ham for the cracklin's and fat.

When I was a kid I
used to get
Uncle Remus
mixed up with
Santa Claus 'cause
stories
is 'bout all I
used to get
for my stockin'
bein' left empty.

Peanut Butter Biscuits

2 cups sifted flour	2 tablespoons lard or other cooking fat
2 teaspoons double-acting or 4 teaspoons single-acting baking powder	2 tablespoons peanut butter
$^1/_2$ teaspoon salt	Milk

Combine the flour, baking powder, and salt and sift together into mixing bowl. Cut in the lard with pastry blender, fork, two knives, or fingertips. Work in the peanut butter, but leave it in pieces. Add enough milk to make a dough that is soft but easy to handle. Turn out onto a lightly floured surface and knead very gently for a minute or less. Pat or roll out to a $^1/_2$" thickness and cut into rounds with biscuit cutter. Place on greased baking sheet about 1" apart and bake at 450°F until golden brown—about 12 to 15 minutes. Serve hot. Makes about 1 dozen.

Lotsa times you kin tell what
a man do by how
he eat. Doctors give
everything a careful
examination first.
Like the lawyers
ready to make a
Federal case outa
everythin' on the plate.
That's the professional
class of eaters.
Artists of all kinds, singers,
actresses, writers, painters,
they the
happiest eaters.
But they always puttin'
on some kind of show.
The best eaters
is the workin'
people, yuh kin see the
pleasure of fillin'
their hunger right on
their faces.

Yam Biscuits

2 cups sifted flour	$^1/_4$ cup lard or other
3 teaspoons double-	shortening
acting baking powder	$^1/_2$ cup grated raw yams
1 teaspoon salt	Milk

Combine the sifted flour, baking powder, and salt and sift together into mixing bowl. Cut in the lard with pastry blender, fork, two knives, or fingertips. Add the grated yams and mix just enough to distribute evenly. Add enough milk to make a dough that is soft but easy to handle and not sticky. Turn out onto lightly floured surface and knead very gently for about 30 seconds. Then lightly roll out to a $^1/_2$" thickness and cut into small squares. Arrange on greased baking sheet about 1" apart and bake at 450°F until done—about 12 minutes. Makes about 1$^1/_2$ dozen.

*I notice that the
people always sayin'
that work never killed
nobody, is got
the time to
sit aroun' and talk
about it.*

Buttermilk Rolls

2 tablespoons shortening*	¹/₂ teaspoon baking powder
1 tablespoon sugar	¹/₂ teaspoon baking soda
1 package dry yeast	¹/₂ teaspoon salt
¹/₄ cup warm water	2¹/₂ cups flour (about)
³/₄ cup buttermilk	

Cream together the shortening and sugar. Stir yeast into warm water in a cup until dissolved and fill with the buttermilk. Let stand for 5 minutes. Sift together the dry ingredients. Stir yeast mixture into shortening. Mix in gradually the dry ingredients. Work in enough flour to make a dough that is soft but firm enough to handle. Turn out onto floured surface and knead until the dough is smooth and elastic. Shape into desired rolls** and let rise until double—about 1 to 1¹/₂ hours. Bake at 400°F until golden brown. Makes about 1¹/₂ dozen.

 EDITORS' NOTES: *Unsalted butter or Crisco. **Divide dough into 12 to 18 equal pieces before flattening and rolling into a cylinder.

Older folks is wiser and thinks
they is stupid
'cause they didn't do it better.
Younger folks ain't tried
it yet and thinks
they know it all.
I think it's jus'
a matter of
puttin' old batter
in new pans.

Corn Bread Fritters

1 cup corn meal	½ teaspoon salt
1 cup flour	1 egg
2 teaspoons baking powder	Milk

Sift together the dry ingredients. Stir in the egg and add enough milk to make a stiff batter. Drop from spoon into deep hot fat* and fry until golden brown. Drain on absorbent paper.

 EDITORS' NOTE: *"Deep hot fat" refers to an inch or more depth of any frying medium, including vegetable, peanut, corn, or canola oil; lard; or any combination thereof. For extra flavor, a piece of salt pork or bark off a country ham can be added to season the oil.

*Every woman should learn
to cook for her man
'cuz love and indigestion
don't mix.*

RICE FRITTERS

1 cup flour	Few grains of salt
1 cup sugar	2 eggs, separated
2 teaspoons baking powder	1 cup cold cooked rice
	$^1/_8$ teaspoon cinnamon

Sift together the flour, sugar, baking powder, and salt. Beat egg yolks until thick. Stir in the flour mixture, rice, and cinnamon. Beat egg whites until stiff and fold into rice mixture. Drop from a tablespoon into deep hot fat and fry until golden brown. Drain on absorbent paper and serve hot, with syrup or molasses or sprinkled with sugar. Serves 6.

Integrate, Integrate,
some people is
always hollerin'.
Separate, Separate
says others.
They so busy integratin'
and separatin' that
it's jus' plain aggravatin'!
The best kind of cookin'
is free to mix in
any ingredients.
So let's
stop talkin' and start
cookin'.

OKRA FRITTERS

1 quart fresh okra, stemmed	2 teaspoons baking powder
Salt and pepper	Flour
2 eggs, beaten	

Cook the okra in boiling water until tender. Drain well and mash.
Season to taste with salt and pepper. Beat in the eggs, baking powder,
and enough flour to make a stiff batter. Drop by the tablespoon* into
deep fat and fry until crisp. Drain on absorbent paper and serve at once.

EDITORS' NOTES: *A precise tablespoon (not a heaping tablespoon). Makes about
100 fritters. Season the finished fritters with a light sprinkling of salt.

*The West cain't
be much of a place for cookin'.
Ain't never seen a fat cowboy.*

Green Corn Griddle Cakes

¹/₂ cup corn meal	2 cups corn cut from cooked tender green corn on the cob
¹/₂ cup flour	
¹/₂ teaspoon baking powder	2 eggs, separated
¹/₂ teaspoon baking soda	³/₄ cup sour milk
2 tablespoons sugar	2 tablespoons melted butter or oleo
¹/₂ teaspoon salt	

Sift together the dry ingredients and add to the corn. Stir in beaten egg yolks, then the sour milk, then the melted butter or oleo. Beat egg whites until stiff and fold in. Cook on hot greased griddle until nicely browned on both sides, turning once. Serve with molasses or syrup. Serves 6.

I'm gonna make me
a flag with a
Christmas tree on it
and declare the
Little Kitchen
neutral territory.
Like Monaco, this
is gonna be
Princess Pamela's
Kingdom Come
and the only passport
anyone is gonna
need, is lovin'
kindness and
a good appetite
for soul cookin'.

BUCKWHEAT CAKES

1 package dry yeast	$1/2$ teaspoon salt
$1/2$ cup warm water	1 tablespoon molasses
2 cups buttermilk	$1/4$ cup melted butter
1 cup flour	1 teaspoon baking soda
2 cups buckwheat flour	$1/2$ cup water

Dissolve the yeast in the warm water and stir in the buttermilk. Sift together the dry ingredients and add to buttermilk mixture. Let rise overnight. In the morning, give the dough a good, vigorous punch. Stir in the molasses, melted butter, and baking soda, which has been dissolved in $1/2$ cup water. Stir hard. Bake on hot griddle. Serve with molasses or syrup and links. Makes about 2 dozen large griddle cakes.

You bein' serious about
what I would wish for
if I had three wishes?
I'd wish for
everyone to have
Peace—Lovin' Kindness—
and the time to
finish
my good cookin'
without runnin'
like the blazes.

Corn Meal Waffles

1 cup corn meal	$^1/_2$ teaspoon salt
1 cup sifted flour	3 eggs, separated
2 teaspoons baking powder	1 tablespoon melted bacon fat
$^1/_2$ teaspoon baking soda	Buttermilk or sour milk

Sift together the dry ingredients. Add the egg yolks and melted bacon fat and beat well. Add enough buttermilk or sour milk to make a thin batter. Beat egg whites until stiff and fold into the batter. Bake in hot, greased waffle iron. Serve with molasses.

The other day somebody
showed me a cookbook for pets.
Now I really do believe the
    world
is goin' to the dogs.

HUSH PUPPIES

2 cups corn meal	$^3/_4$ teaspoon salt
1 tablespoon flour	1 teaspoon sugar
1 teaspoon baking powder	1 egg, well beaten
$^1/_2$ teaspoon baking soda	1 cup buttermilk

Combine the dry ingredients. Add the egg, then the buttermilk, and mix well. Shape into little cakes or drop by the tablespoonful into deep hot fat. Fry until golden brown. Drain on absorbent paper and serve very hot. Makes about 1$^1/_2$ dozen.

One thing I hate,
detest, and abominate is
when folks bring
chillun into the world
and let them run aroun'
in the streets like
stray dogs.
People got to get a
license to get married. They
ought to have a
license to
have kids.

Suet Dumplings

1¹/₂ cups flour

2 teaspoons
  baking powder

1 teaspoon salt

¹/₂ cup finely chopped suet

Milk

Sift together the dry ingredients and blend in the suet. Stir in just enough milk so that the mixture holds together and can be taken up with a spoon and dropped. Drop by spoonfuls on top of boiling beef stew or other dishes. (Do not drop into liquid*.) Cook, uncovered, for 10 minutes. Then cover and cook for 10 minutes more.

 EDITORS' NOTE: *She means to emphasize that your stew should be thick enough to support the dumplings, so they don't sink.

SOUL
GOO

FUL
DIES

A man is stronger but a woman
  kin last longer.
There's a song tells it that goes
like this:
"Six times she married,
that mammy of mine.
Six men, wide as oaks,
she put down in the ground
with lots of weepin'
and holiday funerals
and the best eatin'
that Memphis ever saw."

SWEET POTATO PIE

2 medium-sized sweet
  potatoes, boiled and
  mashed*

1 cup sugar, more or less to
  taste

3 eggs, well beaten

¼ cup melted butter

³/₄ cup milk

1 teaspoon vanilla flavoring

Pinch each of cinnamon and
  nutmeg**

1 tablespoon sifted flour

1 9" pie shell, unbaked

Mix together all the ingredients and pour into unbaked pie shell. Bake
at 400°F until browned—about 35 minutes***.

 EDITORS' NOTES: *1¹/₃ *pounds sweet potatoes, peeled, sliced thick, and boiled for 20 to*
25 minutes. **Add a pinch of salt, too, to the batter.* ***Allow pie to cool and firm for about*
10 minutes before serving.

Peach Skillet Pie

Baking-powder biscuit dough for 9" skillet, rolled out ¹/₄" thick

6 to 8 fresh peaches, peeled, pitted, and sliced

¹/₂ to ³/₄ cup brown or white sugar, depending on sweetness of peaches

1 tablespoon flour

¹/₂ teaspoon salt

¹/₂ teaspoon cinnamon

¹/₄ teaspoon nutmeg

1 tablespoon butter

Place the dough in a heavy 9" skillet, allowing some of it to hang over the edge. Fill with the sliced peaches. Mix together the sugar, flour, salt, cinnamon, and nutmeg. Sprinkle over the peaches and dot with butter. Fold the hanging dough toward the center, leaving a small space in the center for steam to escape. Bake at 450°F for about 25 minutes. Serves 6 to 8.

*These two young
people, they
had an
argument at
my place and
he walk out.
She keep on cryin'
and eatin'.
Eatin' and cryin'.
I never saw nobody
cry so much or
eat so much in
all my born days.*

MOLASSES PECAN PIE

³/₄ cup dark molasses

¹/₂ cup sugar, brown
   or granulated

1 tablespoon vinegar

3 eggs, well beaten

¹/₄ teaspoon nutmeg

¹/₄ teaspoon
   ground allspice

2 tablespoons hot
   melted butter

¹/₂ cup chopped pecans

2 tablespoons rolled
   cracker crumbs

1 8" pie shell, unbaked

Combine the molasses, sugar, and vinegar and boil together for about
2 minutes. Remove from heat and slowly pour over the beaten eggs,
stirring constantly. Beat until smooth and stir in remaining ingredients.
Turn into unbaked pie shell and bake at 300°F for about 35 to 40 minutes.

BROWN COCONUT PIE

1 large coconut, grated
   with its inner
   brown skin

2 cups white granulated
   sugar

1 cup brown sugar

3 eggs, beaten

1 cup milk

1 teaspoon
   vanilla flavoring

1 9" pie shell, unbaked

Combine the coconut, white and brown sugar, eggs, and milk in top of
a double boiler. Cook over hot water for 15 minutes, stirring constantly.
Add vanilla and pour into pie shell. Bake at 375°F until brown*.

EDITORS' NOTES: *30 to 40 minutes. Allow to cool 15 minutes before serving and top
with whipped cream.

*Everybody ask
me how come
I kin do all
my cookin'
in that closet-
space kitchen.
For anyone been in as
many tight spots
as I have,
sweetheart, it's easy
as buttermilk pie.*

BUTTERMILK PIE

3 eggs, separated	2 cups buttermilk
2 cups sugar	1 tablespoon lemon juice
1/2 cup butter	1/2 teaspoon nutmeg
4 tablespoons flour	1 9" pie shell, unbaked

Cream together the egg yolks, sugar, and butter thoroughly. Add the flour and beat. Stir in the buttermilk and lemon juice. Beat the egg whites until stiff and fold into the buttermilk mixture. Add nutmeg and pour into pie shell. Bake at 300°F until firm—about 45 to 50 minutes.

ORANGE PIE

3 eggs	1 cup fresh orange juice
1 cup sugar	1 tablespoon fresh lemon juice
3 tablespoons flour	Grated rind of 1 orange
1 tablespoon butter, melted	1 9" pie shell, unbaked

Blend the eggs well but do not beat. Stir in the remaining ingredients and pour into pie shell. Bake at 350°F until firm—about 35 to 40 minutes.

*I don't want no perfect man.
A man like that gonna
make me look awful bad!*

SOUTHERN CHESS PIE

1 cup brown sugar (packed)	2 eggs, unbeaten
1/2 cup granulated white sugar	1/2 cup melted butter
1 tablespoon flour or corn meal	2 tablespoons milk
	1 teaspoon vanilla
	1 8" pie shell, unbaked

Mix together the brown and white sugar and the flour or corn meal. Break in the eggs. Add the butter, milk, and vanilla and beat. Pour into pie shell and bake at 325°F for about 40 minutes. Cool.

LEMON PIE

1 1/2 cups sugar	1/4 cup butter, melted
1 tablespoon flour	1/4 cup fresh lemon juice
1 tablespoon yellow corn meal	2 tablespoons grated lemon rind
1/4 cup milk	1 9" pie shell, unbaked
4 eggs	

Combine the sugar, flour, and corn meal. Stir in remaining ingredients and beat until smooth. Pour into pie shell and bake at 400°F for about 45 minutes. To test for doneness, insert a knife in the center of pie; when it comes out clean, the pie is done.

Mosey grab my peanuts and
   quick-like,
threw them into the water,
repeatin' the words of the
Reverend's sermon earlier that
   mornin'.
"Cast yore bread upon the
waters and it shall return to ye
a hundredfold."
I kept him standin' there
waiting until after
seven, and when nuthin'
   happened
I started beatin' the daylights
outa him. "Bread," I said
to him, "you damn fool—not
peanuts."

PEANUT PIE

4 eggs, well beaten	3 tablespoons sifted flour
1 cup dark corn syrup	¹/₄ teaspoon salt
¹/₂ cup white sugar	1 cup roasted peanuts
2 tablespoons melted shortening	1 9" pie shell, unbaked

To the beaten eggs, add corn syrup, sugar, shortening, flour, and salt.
Blend thoroughly. Fold in the nuts and pour into unbaked pie shell.
Bake at 350°F for about 30 to 40 minutes.

COCONUT PIE

3 eggs	1 cup freshly grated coconut
1 cup sugar	1 8" pie shell, unbaked
2 tablespoons butter	

Beat the eggs well with the sugar and butter. Add the coconut and pour
into pie shell. Bake at 300°F until firm.

That man do all of his courtin'
right about *the dinner hour.*

RHUBARB PIE

3 cups rhubarb, cut up
1 cup sugar
¹⁄₃ cup cold water
1 tablespoon cornstarch

2 egg yolks
Pastry for double-crust
   9" pie
1 teaspoon butter

Mix the rhubarb with sugar and half the water. Dissolve cornstarch
in remaining water. Add to the rhubarb mixture along with the egg
yolks and mix well. Line a 9" pie plate with crust and fill with rhubarb
mixture. Dot with butter. Top with the second crust, seal the edges, and
prick the top with a fork. Bake at 450°F until rhubarb is cooked—about
30 to 35 minutes.

SOUTHERN FRIED FRUIT PIES

2 cups flour, sifted
1/2 teaspoon salt
1 teaspoon baking soda
1/2 cup lard or vegetable shortening

Ice water
Desired fruit filling*
Powdered sugar (optional)
Fat for frying

Combine flour, salt, and baking soda and sift together into mixing bowl. With pastry blender, fork, two knives, or fingertips, cut in the lard. Sprinkle ice water over the flour mixture by tablespoonfuls, mixing lightly, until enough has been added so that the dough can be shaped into a ball. (Handle the pastry as little as possible.) Wrap the ball in waxed paper and chill. Roll out and cut into rounds with cookie cutter. Place about 2 or 3 tablespoonfuls (depending on size of rounds) of fruit filling in the center of each round. Wet the edge with cold water, fold over, and press with a fork to seal. Fry in deep hot fat until golden brown all over. Drain on absorbent paper. Dust with powdered sugar if desired. Serve hot or cold.

*FRUIT FILLING: Cook the fruit of your choice (such as apples, apricots, peaches) until thick. Add sugar and spices (nutmeg, cinnamon, allspice, etc.) to taste. Canned fruit (such as blueberries, sliced peaches, apricots) may also be used. Sweeten to taste and sprinkle with 2 or 3 tablespoons of minute tapioca to absorb juice.

I won first prize
with my bakin'
and every woman ask for my
*   pecan pie recipe*
and every man for my home
*   address.*

Pecan Pie

1 9" pie shell, unbaked	2 tablespoons flour
2 cups pecans, chopped	1 teaspoon vanilla
1 cup sugar, brown or white	$^1/_4$ teaspoon salt
1 cup light corn syrup	3 eggs
	2 tablespoons butter

Line the pie shell with chopped pecans. Combine the sugar, corn syrup, flour, vanilla, and salt and mix until blended. Beat in the eggs, one at a time, mixing well after each addition. Pour into the nut-lined pie shell and dot with butter. Bake at 350°F until firm—about 1 hour.

APPLE PIE

Pastry for double-crust 9" pie	$^1/_4$ teaspoon cinnamon
6 tart apples, pared, cored, and sliced	$^1/_8$ teaspoon nutmeg
$^1/_2$ cup sugar, brown or white	1 teaspoon lemon juice
	$^1/_4$ teaspoon grated lemon rind
	1 tablespoon butter

Line a 9" pie plate with pastry. Fill with the apples. Combine the dry ingredients with lemon juice and rind and sprinkle over the apples. Dot with butter. Cover with top crust. Moisten the edges with water and press together. Trim the edges and prick the top crust with a fork. Bake at 450°F until fruit is cooked—about 40 to 45 minutes.

A woman runnin' a business got no business lettin' a man run her. It become a hand-to-mouth existence, with her hand to his mouth.

Molasses Pie

1 cup molasses
1/4 cup sugar, brown or
   granulated
4 tablespoons butter
3 eggs, well beaten
1 teaspoon flour

1 teaspoon
   vanilla flavoring
1 cup chopped
   pecans (optional)
1 8" pie shell, unbaked

Combine the molasses, sugar, butter, eggs, flour, and vanilla. Cook
and stir in the top of a double boiler until all the ingredients are well
blended. Fold in the nuts (optional) and pour into pie shell. Bake at
300°F for about 35 to 40 minutes.

ANGEL PIE

4 egg whites
1 cup sugar
1/2 teaspoon baking
   powder
1/4 teaspoon salt

1/2 teaspoon vanilla
   flavoring
Filling
Whipped cream

Beat the egg whites until stiff. Beat in, a little at a time, the sugar, baking
powder, salt, and vanilla. Spread in a buttered 9" pie pan, allowing the
mixture to stand higher than the edge of the pan. Bake at 250°F until firm
and dry but not brown—about 1 1/2 hours. Cool. Fill with your favorite
coconut, lemon, or orange filling or with sweetened raspberries or halved
strawberries. Cover with a layer of whipped cream.

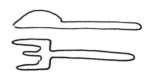

*Oh, that man, he's
a swinger with
a knife 'n fork!*

Sweet Potato Tarts

Pastry for double-crust
 8" pie

1³/₄ cups mashed cooked
 sweet potatoes

2 tablespoons butter or
 oleo, melted

²/₃ cup brown
 sugar (packed)

1 teaspoon cinnamon

¹/₂ teaspoon mace
 or nutmeg

¹/₄ teaspoon ginger

¹/₄ teaspoon ground cloves

¹/₂ teaspoon salt

3 eggs, separated

1¹/₄ cups milk

Divide the pastry dough into 8 equal parts. Roll out each part and fit into individual pie or tart pans. Combine the sweet potatoes, butter or oleo, brown sugar, spices, salt, egg yolks, and milk. Beat together until smooth and well blended. Beat the egg whites until stiff and fold into the sweet potato mixture. Pour into the tart shells. Bake at 425°F for 20 minutes, then lower heat to 375°F and continue baking for about 20 minutes more.

Southern Lemon Curd

The ingredients are: six eggs, 1 pound of sugar, ¼ pound of butter, the juice of 3 medium-sized lemons, the grated rind of 2 lemons, and a pinch of salt. Melt the butter in the top of a double boiler. Stir in the sugar, lemon juice, grated rind, and salt. Beat the eggs slightly and add. Cook over hot water until thick and shiny, stirring frequently. Cool. Store in the refrigerator. Use as cake filling or for pies and tarts.

*The luckiest people in the
world are the ones who
tellya that if they
had it t'do all
over again, they would have
it happen the same way.
For me,
that would be like
askin' for a return
ride through hell.*

Green Tomato Mincemeat

3 cups chopped
green tomatoes

3 cups chopped, pared
cooking apples

1¹/₂ cups seeded raisins

2 cups brown sugar

1 tablespoon molasses

²/₃ cup mild vinegar

Salt and pepper to taste

1¹/₂ teaspoons cinnamon

¹/₄ teaspoon nutmeg

¹/₂ teaspoon ground cloves

¹/₄ teaspoon
ground allspice

¹/₄ teaspoon mace

6 tablespoons butter

Combine all the ingredients, except the butter, in a pot and slowly bring
to the boiling point. Cover and simmer for 3 hours. Add the butter, pour
into jars, seal, and store in a cool place. Makes 3 pints, enough for 3 pies*.

EDITORS' NOTE: *Yield is closer to 2 pints, enough for 1 pie.

PIE PASTRY

2 cups pastry flour

1 teaspoon salt

²/₃ cup lard*

¹/₄ cup ice-cold water

Sift together the flour and salt into mixing bowl. Cut in the lard
with pastry blender, fork, two knives, or fingers. Sprinkle the water,
1 tablespoon at a time, over the flour mixture, stirring just enough to
moisten. Pat the dough into a ball, wrap in waxed paper, and chill. When
ready to use, divide into two parts and roll out. Makes a two-crust 9" pie.

EDITORS' NOTE: *Using all lard, as called for in the recipe, results in a slightly porky
pie pastry; feel free to substitute cold unsalted butter for the lard, or to cut a proportion of the
lard with the same amount of butter.

I may not be the smartest thing ever walked on two feet but you don't have t' point t' the sky t' tell me which way is up. An' nobody kin beat my cobbler, so how far wrong kin I go?

LITTLE KITCHEN SPECIAL

Peach Cobbler

3 cups pared and sliced
  fresh peaches

1 cup sugar

Pinch of salt

1 egg, well beaten

1 teaspoon flour

Butter

Cinnamon

Pie pastry

Combine the peaches, sugar, salt, egg, and flour. Turn into a buttered baking dish. Dot with butter and sprinkle with cinnamon. Roll out the pastry and cut into strips about ½" wide. Place over the fruit to form a lattice top. Bake at 400°F for about 30 minutes. Serve warm.

BLACKBERRY COBBLER

3 cups fresh blackberries	1 cup milk
1¹/₄ cups flour	2 tablespoons butter or oleo
1 cup sugar	¹/₂ teaspoon grated lemon rind
¹/₄ teaspoon salt	¹/₂ teaspoon cinnamon
2¹/₂ teaspoons baking powder	

Prepare the berries. Combine flour, sugar, salt, and baking powder and sift together into mixing bowl. Slowly stir in the milk and beat well. Melt the butter or oleo in a deep baking dish. Pour in the batter. Then add the blackberries and sprinkle with grated lemon rind and cinnamon. Bake at 350°F until golden brown. (The batter will rise to the top and make a nice crust.) Serve warm from the baking dish. Serves 6 to 8.

Note: Blueberries or huckleberries may be substituted for the blackberries.

*When he sit hisself
down to eat,
that big black man,
he take two places
at the table
and nuthin'
I tell you
nuthin' pass him by.*

APPLE DUMPLINGS

1¹/₂ cups flour
2 tablespoons sugar
1 teaspoon salt
¹/₂ cup shortening
Cold milk or water

6 medium-sized cooking
  apples, pared and cored
Brown sugar
Cinnamon
Nutmeg

Combine flour, sugar, and salt and sift together into mixing bowl. Cut in the shortening. Add enough milk or water to make a dough that is soft but easy to handle. Turn out onto floured surface, roll out, and cut into 6 squares. Fill the apple cavities with a mixture of brown sugar, cinnamon, and nutmeg. Place an apple on each square of dough, draw the corners together on top, and pinch the edges together. Bake or steam until apples are tender.

Peach Dumplings

1 cup sugar

1 cup water

6 fresh peaches, pared, pitted, and halved

Cinnamon or nutmeg

1½ cups flour, sifted

1½ teaspoons baking powder

Pinch of salt

2 tablespoons lard*

Milk

Combine sugar and water in saucepan and cook until sugar is dissolved, stirring constantly. Add peaches and cook over low heat until they are almost tender. Sprinkle with cinnamon or nutmeg. Combine flour, baking powder, and salt. Mix well, then cut in the lard. Stir in enough milk, little by little, until a dough is formed that is soft but easy to handle. Drop by spoonfuls on top of the peaches. Cover tightly and continue cooking for about 10 minutes. Serve warm, with milk or cream. Serves 6.

 EDITORS' NOTE: *Unsalted butter makes a fine substitute for the lard in this recipe.*

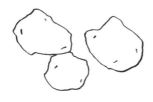

There ain't a thing I do,
a person I know,
a dish I cook,
couldn't be made
a mite better. That's
no reason
not to love it
for the best that it is
right now.

SWEET POTATO CAKE

1¹/₂ cups sifted flour

2 teaspoons baking powder

¹/₄ teaspoon salt

2 cups hot, boiled and mashed sweet potatoes

¹/₂ cup shortening*

2 eggs, well beaten

³/₄ cup brown sugar

¹/₂ teaspoon cinnamon

¹/₂ teaspoon nutmeg

¹/₂ cup milk

1 tablespoon lemon juice

Combine flour, baking powder, and salt and sift into mixing bowl. To the mashed potatoes, add shortening, eggs, brown sugar, cinnamon, and nutmeg. Beat well. Alternately add the flour mixture and milk, beating well after each addition. Add lemon juice and turn into greased loaf pan. Bake at 350°F until done—about 1 hour**.

 EDITORS' NOTES: *Crisco recommended. **About 1 hour and 15 minutes is a better estimate.

LITTLE KITCHEN SPECIAL

RUM CAKE

³/₄ cup butter, softened

2 cups of sugar

4 eggs, separated

2¹/₃ cups sifted cake flour

2 teaspoons
  baking powder

¹/₂ teaspoon salt

³/₄ cup milk

1 teaspoon vanilla

1 teaspoon lemon juice

¹/₄ teaspoon grated
  lemon rind

Raspberry preserves

Rum

Whipped cream

Cream the butter. Add the sugar gradually, creaming the mixture throughout until it is fluffy. Beat the yolks until lemon-yellow and blend into the butter mixture. Sift together the flour, baking powder, and salt. Alternately add the dry ingredients and the milk to the butter mixture, a little at a time and mixing thoroughly. Stir in the vanilla, lemon juice, and grated lemon rind. Beat the egg whites until stiff but not dry. Fold into the batter. Pour into a greased 8" x 12" cake pan and bake at 350°F for about 40 minutes. Cool. Cut the cake in half crosswise. Spread a thin layer of raspberry preserves over the top of one half and place the other half over it. Moisten liberally with rum. Serve in squares, topped with a generous mound of real whipped cream.

*I had two
dolls and I used to
cook for them on
a lil' toy stove.
You could tell right off which
one was
my favorite, 'cause
she was the chubby one
who liked my cookin'
the best.*

SHORTCAKE

2 cups flour	1/3 cup shortening
3 teaspoons baking powder	Milk
2 tablespoons sugar	Butter
1/2 teaspoon salt	1 quart prepared fruit*

Combine the flour, baking powder, sugar, and salt, and sift together into mixing bowl. With a pastry blender or fingers, cut in the shortening. Stir in milk, a little at a time, until a dough is formed that is soft but easy to handle. Pat the dough into a greased, round 8" cake pan. Dot with 1 tablespoon of butter. Bake at 450°F until nicely browned—about 15 minutes. Carefully split crosswise while hot and spread generously with butter. Place the prepared fruit between layers and on top. Serve warm, with cream. Serves 6.

*Use sweetened raspberries or sliced strawberries; sliced sugared peaches or bananas; stewed sweetened blueberries; or warm applesauce.

Molasses Cake

¹/₂ pound (1 cup) butter

1 cup sugar, brown
   or white

3 eggs

1 teaspoon baking soda

1 cup molasses

3 cups flour

¹/₂ teaspoon cinnamon

¹/₂ teaspoon ginger

¹/₄ teaspoon ground cloves

¹/₄ teaspoon nutmeg

1 cup milk

¹/₂ cup floured
   raisins (optional)

Cream together the butter and sugar, then beat in the eggs. Add baking soda to the molasses. Combine flour with spices and sift. Alternately add molasses, flour mixture, and milk to the egg mixture. Add raisins if desired. Turn into a loaf pan and bake at 350°F for about 45 minutes.

*She was a big woman and weary.
Bone-weary from
washin' other folks' floors and
woodwork so clean you
could eat rice pudding off of it.*

RICE PUDDING

4 cups milk
2 eggs, beaten
1/2 cup molasses
1/2 cup raw brown rice

1/2 teaspoon cinnamon
1/8 teaspoon salt
2 tablespoons butter

Mix together the milk, eggs, molasses, rice, cinnamon, and salt. Pour
into a casserole or baking dish. Bake, uncovered, at 275°F for 3 hours.
Stir several times during the first hour of cooking. Add the butter
during the final stirring. If desired, stir in 1/4 cup raisins or chopped figs
after the first hour of cooking. Serves 4 to 6.

Skillet Sweet Potato Pudding

²/₃ cup butter

4 cups coarsely grated raw
  sweet potatoes

1¹/₂ cups molasses

¹/₂ cup brown sugar

1 cup milk

2 tablespoons flour

1 teaspoon ground allspice

¹/₂ teaspoon cinnamon

¹/₂ teaspoon nutmeg

¹/₂ teaspoon ginger

1 teaspoon grated
  orange rind

2 eggs, beaten

Melt the butter in a heavy iron skillet*. Combine the grated sweet potatoes with the molasses, brown sugar, milk, flour, spices, and orange rind, adding the eggs last. Blend thoroughly and stir into the melted butter in skillet. Cook on top of the stove, stirring occasionally, until quite thick. Then place in the oven until nicely browned on top.

EDITORS' NOTE: *A 10-inch skillet is ideal.

There was a minister used to
come 'round to
my place and eat my bread
puddin'
like there was no tomorrow—
never
havin' room to eat anythin' else.
So this one time he come into
my place
I served him up a big plate of
ribs, chicken, black-eyed peas,
and
collard greens, and a little
sign, sayin'—"Man doth
not live by bread puddin'
alone."

BREAD PUDDING

3 cups milk

$^{1}/_{4}$ cup butter or oleo

4 cups soft bread crumbs

2 eggs, slightly beaten

$^{1}/_{2}$ cup sugar

$^{1}/_{3}$ teaspoon salt

1 teaspoon
   vanilla flavoring

Cinnamon or nutmeg

Scald the milk with the butter or oleo. Add the bread crumbs. Then stir in the beaten eggs, sugar, salt, and vanilla. Pour the mixture into a baking dish or casserole and sprinkle with cinnamon or nutmeg. Set in a pan of hot water and bake at 325°F until an inserted knife comes out clean—about 1 hour. Serve warm, plain or with cream. Serves 6.

LITTLE KITCHEN SPECIAL

BREAD PUDDING
WITH FRUIT SAUCE

4 cups 2-day-old bread,
cut in 1" cubes

1 quart hot milk

3 eggs

³/₄ cup sugar

¹/₂ teaspoon salt

1 teaspoon cinnamon

¹/₂ teaspoon nutmeg

2 teaspoons vanilla,
or 1 teaspoon
almond extract

2 tablespoons
butter, melted

Fruit Sauce*

Stir bread cubes into the hot milk and set aside. Butter a casserole or baking dish. Break the eggs into it and beat slightly. Stir in the sugar, salt, bread-milk mixture, cinnamon, nutmeg, extract, and butter. Set in a pan of hot water and bake at 350°F for about 1 hour. Serve warm or cold, with Fruit Sauce. Serves 6.

*FRUIT SAUCE: Crush fresh peaches, raspberries, or strawberries and sweeten to taste with sugar. Flavor with vanilla or almond extract or a liqueur such as kirsch or cognac.

*Some faces
you see for a minute
and they stay with
yuh all yore
life. Lady once stop
me on the
street when I was
twelve or thirteen.
She
put her hand on my
head and tell me
everythin' goin' to
turn out good if
I be decent and
keep the word.
Every time since
I had bad trouble
I would
see her face.*

GRITS PUDDING

1 cup cooked hominy grits (see page 141)

1 tablespoon butter or oleo

2 cups hot milk

¹/₄ cup sugar

¹/₄ teaspoon salt

¹/₃ cup raisins, chopped figs, or chopped pecans

Pinch of cinnamon (optional)

2 eggs, well beaten

Stir grits and butter or oleo into the hot milk. Add the sugar, salt, raisins, figs or nuts, and cinnamon to the eggs. Slowly stir into the hot milk mixture. Pour into greased casserole or baking dish and set in a pan of hot water. Bake at 350°F until set—about 1 hour. Serves 4.

APPLE SAUCE

Wash and quarter cooking apples, allowing 1 to 2 apples per serving, depending on their size. Place in a saucepan with about ¹/₂" of water and add a pinch of salt. Cover and simmer until apples are tender. Then put them through a coarse strainer or a food mill. Sweeten to taste with sugar and simmer gently for a few more minutes. If the apples are not sufficiently tart, add several drops of lemon juice. If desired, season with cinnamon, nutmeg, or mace.

*I was 'bout
four or five
when I learned
to bake cookies,
and the way kids would
line up
at the kitchen
door, you'd
a thought
it was the U. S. Mint
and I was givin'
away nickels.*

SHORT'NIN' BREAD

2 cups (1 pound) butter or oleo	4 cups flour
1 cup light brown sugar	Few grains of salt

Cream the butter or oleo. Add and blend in the sugar. Add flour and salt and work thoroughly with hands until smooth. Chill. Then roll out ½" thick and cut into squares. Arrange on ungreased cookie sheet and bake at 325°F for about 25 minutes.

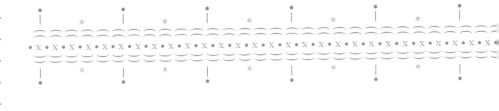

SOUTHERN DOUGHNUTS

¹/₄ cup butter	1 teaspoon baking soda
1 cup sugar	¹/₂ teaspoon salt
3 eggs, well beaten	¹/₂ teaspoon nutmeg
3¹/₂ cups sifted flour (about)	1 cup sour milk or buttermilk
2 teaspoons baking powder	

Cream together butter and sugar. Stir in the eggs. Sift together the flour, baking powder, baking soda, salt, and nutmeg. Alternately add flour mixture and the milk to egg mixture. Add more flour if necessary to make the dough firm enough to handle. Turn out onto floured board and roll out to ¹/₃" thickness. Let stand for 20 minutes. Cut out with floured doughnut cutter and fry in deep hot lard or substitute until brown. Drain on absorbent paper.

CONVERSION CHART

All conversions are approximate.

LIQUID

U.S	METRIC
1 tsp	5 ml
1 tbsp	15 ml
2 tbsp	30 ml
3 tbsp	45 ml
1/4 cup	60 ml
1/3 cup + 2 tbsp	100 ml
1/2 cup	120 ml
2/3 cup	150 ml
3/4 cup	180 ml
3/4 cup + 2 tbsp	200 ml
1 cup	240 ml
1 cup + 2 tbsp	275 ml
1 1/4 cups	300 ml
1 1/3 cups	325 ml
1 1/2 cups	350 ml
1 2/3 cups	375 ml
1 3/4 cups	400 ml
1 3/4 cups + 2 tbsp	450 ml
2 cups (1 pint)	475 ml
2 1/2 cups	600 ml
3 cups	720 ml
4 cups (1 quart)	945 ml

WEIGHT

U.S. / U.K.	METRIC
1/2 oz	14 g
1 oz	28 g
1 1/2 oz	43 g
2 oz	57 g
2 1/2 oz	71 g
3 oz	85 g
3 1/2 oz	100 g
4 oz	113 g
5 oz	142 g
6 oz	170 g
7 oz	200 g
8 oz	227 g
9 oz	255 g
10 oz	284 g
11 oz	312 g
12 oz	340 g
13 oz	368 g
14 oz	400 g
15 oz	425 g
1 lb	454 g

TEMPERATURE

°F	GAS MARK	°C
250	1/2	120
275	1	140
300	2	150
325	3	165
350	4	180
375	5	190
400	6	200
425	7	220
450	8	230
475	9	240
500	10	260
550	Broil	290

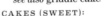

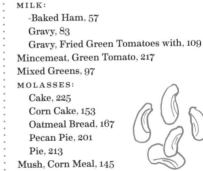

EPILOGUE

Working on this reissue of Pamela Strobel's book, we encountered many people with fond and vivid memories of Princess Pamela. Yet even her closest acquaintances are at a loss to explain where she may be now, or what happened to her after the restaurant closed around 1998. During the course of our research, we hired genealogists and a private investigator to look into records in New York and in her hometown of Spartanburg, South Carolina, and we learned more about her early life, but nothing about the latter years. (She was likely born "Addie" Strobel, in 1928 or 1929; her mother, "Beauty," went by "Rosella" in the U.S. Census and died in 1939.) The only people she was closely associated with were Ada Spivey, an employee at the restaurant (whom we cannot locate), and Bobby Vidal, a bandleader and jazz bassist who died in 1997. She may not have had children. We still hold out hope that someone knows what happened to Pamela Strobel, and it would be gratifying if the publication of this book brought that information to light. If you have any leads—or would like to add your own testimony, tribute, photos, or ephemera from an experience with Princess Pamela—please visit princesspamela.org or send an email to iremberprincess@princesspamela.org

Menu:

B.Q. Ribs =	2.75
Meat Loaf =	2.00
Liver (Smothered (with) Onions =	2.25
Fried Chicken = (Southern Style) =	2.25
Pork Chops (Smothered (with) Onions =	2.80
Fried Fish =	2.95
Oxtail (Ragou) =	2.25
Vegetable Plate (Greens, Rice, Yams Salad & Corn Bread	2.00

"Vegetable's"

Collard Greens •
Black eye Peas •
Salad Beautiful •
Steamed Rice •
Home Made Potatoe Salad •
Yams

Extra Veg. = .35
Yams (or) Salad Beautiful = .45

Hot Corn Bread Serred
with Meals
Extra Corn Bread = .20

"Reservation
Prefered."